What I **Wish I Knew** at 18

STUDENT GUIDE

CHRISTIAN EDITION

What I
Wish
I Knew
at 18

STUDENT GUIDE, CHRISTIAN EDITION

LIFE LESSONS FOR
THE ROAD AHEAD

DENNIS TRITTIN
ARLYN LAWRENCE

LifeSmart

PUBLISHING

What I Wish I Knew at 18: Life Lessons for the Road Ahead – Student Guide, Christian Edition
First Edition Student Guide—Christian Edition, 2011
Copyright © 2011 by Dennis Trittin

Unless otherwise noted, all Scripture quotations taken from the Holy Bible, New Living Translation,
copyright © 1996. Used by permission of Tyndale House Publishers, Inc., Wheaton, Illinois 60189.

Scriptures marked NIV are taken from the Holy Bible, New International Version®, copyright © 1973,
1978, 1984 International Bible Society. All rights reserved throughout the world. Used by permission of
International Bible Society.

Published by LifeSmart Publishing, LLC. Gig Harbor, WA 98332.

Additional guides can be purchased through LifeSmart Publishing.
To Order:
www.dennistrittin.com
info@dennistrittin.com
www.atlasbooks.com

ISBN: 978-0-9832526-6-5
Editorial: Dennis Trittin, Arlyn Lawrence
Book Packaging: Scribe Book Company, Lawton, OK
Cover Design: Susan Browne, Nashville, TN
Book Design: Paul Gant
Composition: PerfecType, Nashville, TN
Printed in the USA by Bookmasters, Ashland, OH

CONTENTS

INTRODUCTION

Welcome to the accompanying study guide for *What I Wish I Knew at 18: Life Lessons for the Road Ahead*. Many, if not most of you, have never taken a course of study quite like this. That's because the book and this guide are completely unique! They're meant to give you a before-the-fact glimpse of the "real world" and what you need to soar into adulthood with confidence, character, and purpose.

This edition of the *What I Wish I Knew at 18* course was written particularly for those students who are embarking on their life journey with a Christian perspective. Knowing that God has a plan and purpose for your life is a great foundation for building a life of impact. His Word provides invaluable and trustworthy principles for developing your worldview and life perspective—the foundation from which everything else in your life will grow.

A Christian worldview, in particular, is an understanding of reality foundationally based on the Bible. It is a belief in a personal, transcendent God who created the universe and mankind, and who has a vested interest and involvement in the significance of each and every person in this world—including YOU!

Your worldview is important, and it pays to be mindful of it. We hope this course will help you think about and develop it strategically. We also hope you'll learn and begin to apply effective methods and practices of successful and honorable leaders who will help you live wisely and productively . . . to achieve your personal best at life!

In order to get the most out of this study, it's essential to be totally honest with yourself—about your strengths *and* areas for improvement. You will no doubt feel stretched outside of your comfort zone at times, but that's what personal growth is all about! At the same time, you will have ample opportunities to demonstrate your strengths and help others with your constructive feedback. You will be working in teams throughout your life and this will give you excellent preparation. So, take it seriously, be yourself, and help your group by being a great team player.

May the book and this accompanying study guide help successfully launch you to amazing heights in the "real world" as you discover—and fulfill—God's amazing purpose for and call on your life!

Dennis Trittin

Arlyn Lawrence

Gig Harbor, Washington
September, 2011

Chapter 1—**LIFE PERSPECTIVE**

Discover your purpose and inspiration * Build a living legacy * Direct your life toward others * **Live life without regrets** * **Don't define success by riches** * **Diversify your life** * Don't allow work to consume your life * Plan, practice, and persevere to succeed * Take risks—even if you might fail * See the glass as half full * Control what you can, but accept what you can't * Value the ride, not just the outcome * Embrace change as an opportunity * **Commit to being a lifelong learner** * Allow time to reflect * Immerse yourself in the beauty of God's creation

> *Thank you for making me so wonderfully complex! Your workmanship is marvelous—how well I know it. . . . You saw me before I was born. Every day of my life was recorded in your book. Every moment was laid out before a single day had passed. How precious are your thoughts about me, O God. They cannot be numbered! I can't even count them; they outnumber the grains of sand! —Psalm 139: 14–18a*

Did you know that you were *created* for purpose? No matter the place, the timing, or even the circumstances of your birth, you were no accident. The Bible says in Psalm 139 (above) that before you were even born, God knew you and had a plan and purpose for the person you would become. Now that's incredible!

You are now at an important and exciting juncture in your life—discovering just who that person—YOU—really is and is meant to become! Your life ahead is like an open road, and you'll be making many decisions that will define your destination and the path you'll take to get there.

Along the way, your philosophical approach to life will have a major impact on the person you become. It will guide your interests and pursuits, the diversity and richness of your experiences, how you define success, and, ultimately, the legacy you will leave. As if that's not enough, your worldview and life perspective also impact your disposition and outlook on life. While your family of origin has played a significant role in forming how you view and relate to the world, much of it is a personal choice that can be developed and refined along the way. Commit to living life with passion, purpose, and confidence in who God created you to be!

OBJECTIVES:

❙ Begin to think about (and eventually identify) some components of your life purpose and why you should have one

❙ Learn about some common life regrets identified by reflective senior citizens that you can determine NOW to avoid

❙ Be able to define and measure success more broadly than in monetary terms

❙ Understand what it means to live a diversified lifestyle and how to create balance and variety in your activities

❙ See the value in being a lifelong learner and identify ways to adopt a passion for learning

Prepare

▌ Read Chapter One ("Life Perspective") in *What I Wish I Knew at 18*, beginning on page 25.

▌ Use your highlighter pen to mark any sections that jump out at you— things you want to remember, take note of, or consider later.

▌ In the chart below, identify the pointers from the chapter you consider to be:

1. the most important in life
2. ones you think you are already doing well and can model to others
3. ones you either find the most challenging or in which you may need guidance to apply to your life

1. the most important in life

2. ones you think you are already doing well and can model to others

3. ones you either find the most challenging or in which you may need guidance to apply to your life

POINTER #1 —
DISCOVER YOUR PURPOSE AND INSPIRATION

 ## Consider

It comes as no surprise that the most successful people are purposeful and goal oriented in the way they live. They apply their skills and abilities to organizations and relationships and accomplish big things in the process. They are committed to making a positive impact and focus their energy on achieving their mission. Their lives have meaning and are rich in fulfillment. They leave powerful legacies and are honored for the difference they made to others.

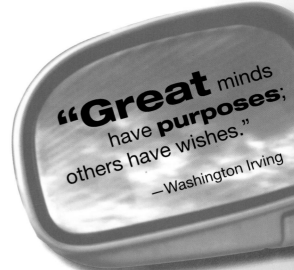

"**Great** minds have **purposes**; others have wishes."

—Washington Irving

Following are some questions to ponder when considering your life purpose. Take a few minutes to fill in the blanks with the first thoughts that come to mind:

▌ What causes am I most passionate about (e.g., global or community needs, people, situations, organizations)? What problems would I most like to solve? What needs or people tug at my heart?

_____

_____

_____

▌ What inspires me the most?

_____

_____

_____

▌ What brings me the greatest joy and sense of fulfillment?

_____

_____

_____

▌ What do I sense God "calling" me to do?

_____

_____

▌ Whose lives do I admire most and why?

_____

_____

▌ What are my special gifts and talents?

_____

_____

▌ Where might my skills have the greatest potential impact?

_____

_____

_____

Once you ponder these questions, see if a picture emerges about a cause or area that could benefit from your unique skill set and experience. Your purpose might be developing inside.

THINK ABOUT THIS!

If you have a purpose in life—lofty or not—you'll live longer, a new study shows. "It can be anything—from wanting to accomplish a goal in life, to achieving something in a volunteer organization, to as little as reading a series of books," said study author Dr. Patricia Boyle, a neuropsychologist and assistant professor of behavioral sciences at Rush University Medical Center in Chicago.[1]

 **Discuss**

In your small group, talk about your answers to the following questions (some may include activities for you to do together). Be honest and respect others' responses. There are no right or wrong answers, and your group should be a safe place to talk freely.

When in your life have you experienced pure joy and fulfillment? How about times when you had a significant impact on something or someone? Do you think those might contribute to identifying your life purpose? Maybe you have a sense that God is "calling" you to some sort of life pursuit or another. Share your impressions with the rest of your small group.

Some people in your group may find it more challenging than others to translate their likes and interests into a life purpose or "calling." Help each other out: as you each relate what makes you feel the happiest or most fulfilled, try and identify different life pursuits for each group member that could be worth exploring.

 **Apply**

1. Tell one person (who doesn't have to be someone in class) a component of what you think your life purpose or calling might be, and why it's important to you. Ask him or her to check back with you from time to time to see whether it still applies, and how you're working toward it. That's called accountability!

2. Watch these two classic movies that illustrate what it looks like to pursue a life calling:
   - *Chariots of Fire* (1981, starring Ben Cross—the story of Eric Liddell, British runner)
   - *Inn of the Sixth Happiness* (1958, starring Ingrid Berman—the story of Gladys Aylward, British missionary to China)

 Words to Live By

"For I know the plans I have for you," says the LORD. "They are plans for good and not for disaster, to give you a future and a hope". —Jeremiah 29:11

POINTER #2 —
LIVE LIFE WITHOUT REGRETS

 Consider

Inevitably, we'll look back at life one day and wish we'd done some things differently. After all, nobody makes it through life being perfect! But that doesn't mean we can't take steps to avoid regrets before they happen.

It's interesting to note what elderly people say they regret the most. In fact, if you ask senior citizens about their life regrets they'll likely tell you some version of the following:

If you already have some regrets, don't be too hard on yourself. It's never too late to get a fresh start.

   1. I didn't spend enough time with my loved ones.
   2. I didn't tell my family and friends I loved them often enough.

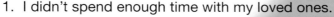

3. I was too stubborn or proud to admit my mistakes and apologize.
4. I chose bitterness over reconciliation.
5. I allowed my life to be consumed by work.
6. I was too hesitant to take risks and try new things.
7. I wasted too much time.
8. I didn't appreciate the little things in life.
9. I valued things over relationships.
10. I worried too much.

Did you notice the common themes? The fact is, *everyone* has regrets. In some cases, they may be based on things you simply wish you'd done differently. If so, you just need to forgive yourself, learn the lesson, and commit to doing better the next time. That's right! Forgive *yourself* for whatever it is that you're regretful of, and let it go. If God can cast our failings as far as the east is from the west (see Psalm 103:8–14), so can you!

In other cases, our regrets stem from our sinful nature. When regrets ARE sin (i.e., something that violates God's Word or character in some way), we have the assurance that if we honestly confront the issue, repent of the sin, and seek God's forgiveness, it's washed away and we do, indeed, get a fresh start. Additionally, if those kinds of regrets involve ways you've hurt other people, God may also want you to take the additional step of going to that person or people, apologizing, and asking for their forgiveness. These can be hard steps to take, but they are incredibly freeing when you follow through with them.

So, if you already have some regrets, don't be too hard on yourself. It's never too late to get a fresh start. Start with asking God to forgive you and to offer you guidance. He is quick (and happy) to do it.

1 John 1:9
But if we confess our sins to him, he is faithful and just to forgive us our sins and to cleanse us . . .

If your regrets are relatively minor, it may be something as easy as making some midcourse corrections and "relationship repairs" along the way. If your regrets are more serious, you may want to consider enlisting the help of a parent, pastor, youth leader, school counselor, or some other trusted mentor who can give you wise counsel and encouragement.

So, how does one live a life with few regrets? The answer is to periodically take a "regret check," pray for God's guidance, and then do something about it, as difficult as it may be.

 **Discuss**

Look again at the list of regrets expressed by senior citizens. Were you surprised? Do you notice how many of them relate to relationships and priorities? Why do you think this is? If you polled a group of eighteen-year-olds, what do you think *their* regrets might be? Make a list in your group.

Apply

Think back on your past year of school. Is there something you wish you would have done differently? Are any relationships in need of repair or rejuvenation? Have you already made positive steps to correct it? If not, come up with a proactive strategy for turning it around— starting today!

Words to Live By

This means that anyone who belongs to Christ has become a new person. The old life is gone; a new life has begun! —2 Corinthians 5:17

I focus on this one thing: Forgetting the past and looking forward to what lies ahead, I press on to reach the end of the race and receive the heavenly prize for which God, through Christ Jesus, is calling us. —Philippians 3:13

POINTER #3 —
DON'T DEFINE SUCCESS BY RICHES

Consider

How will you know if and when you've achieved success in your life? Is there a certain number of dollars you think measures success? How about a certain accomplishment, position, or possession that would make you feel like you'd "made it?"

One need only look at bookshelves, the entertainment industry, the infomercials, and all the free financial seminars to see that our culture defines success in terms of wealth, fame, and power. But, don't you buy it for a minute! Money does *not* buy happiness.

As far as worldly success goes—that is, wealth and all that comes with it—many would agree that the biblical figure Solomon wins hands down. King Solomon was "greater than all the kings of the earth in riches and in wisdom" (1 Kings 10:23). He ruled Israel from about 960 to 922 BC and built a magnificent temple in Jerusalem like none in the world had ever seen.

Before he died, Solomon's father, King David, gave him some advice. Was it to "make the most money you can, play hard, and die happy"? Not even close! King David told Solomon, "Observe the requirements of the LORD your God, and follow all his ways . . . so that *you will be successful in all you do* and wherever you go" (1 Kings 2:3, emphasis added). We shouldn't be surprised, then, that when God later asked Solomon what he would ask for if God would grant him anything, his answer wasn't wealth. Rather, he asked for *wisdom* (see 1 Kings 3:5–14). God was pleased, and He gave it to him . . PLUS God granted him the worldly wealth and success that Solomon *didn't* ask for!

True success starts with valuing the things that God values, not what the world values. Jesus probably said it best when He said, "Seek first (God's) kingdom and his righteousness, and all these things will be given to you as well" (Matthew 6:33, NIV).

True success starts with valuing the things that God values, not what the world values.

So what, exactly, is *real* success? As you're formulating your criteria for what success means to you, consider the following quote by Bessie Stanley in the *Lincoln Sentinel* on November 30, 1905:

> *He has achieved success who has lived well, laughed
> often and loved much; who has gained the respect of intelligent men and
> the love of little children; who has filled his niche and accomplished his task; who has
> left the world better than he found it, whether by an improved poppy, a perfect poem, or
> a rescued soul; who has never lacked appreciation of earth's beauty or failed to express
> it; who has always looked for the best in others and given them the best he had; whose
> life was an inspiration; whose memory a benediction.*

You are in control of how you define success. Rather than basing it on monetary wealth, consider a more comprehensive definition that would include God's perspective and Bessie Stanley's ideals as well as the following:

1. How you applied your gifts, skills, and abilities to the betterment of others
2. The quality of your relationships with people
3. The strength of your character
4. How well you fulfilled your roles as friend, son/daughter, spouse, parent, etc.
5. That you lived for God and others

With all that in mind, how would *you* define a successful life?

 # Discuss

How will you measure success? Each person in the group should come up with at least six criteria for measuring a successful life OTHER THAN MONEY. These can include (but are not limited to) such things as: accomplishing a goal, serving others, proven character, a strong and growing relationship with God, recognition in one's field, health and energy, financial freedom (doesn't necessarily mean wealth), a lifetime marriage, peace of mind, etc. Try to come up with some different ones too. Then compile a complete list using everyone's criteria and share your list with the rest of the class. Synthesize the lists and come up with a top ten list of ways to measure success. How might this list compare with the definitions expressed in the Bible and by Bessie Stanley?

Apply

Make a list of people who exemplify your definition of success. You may identify different people who are successful in different aspects of your definition. For example, in the area of personal character, it may be an extended family member or someone in your community whom you look up to. When it comes to achievement in a chosen field, it may be a famous person. When it comes to spiritual life, it may be a pastor, missionary, or other Christian leader whose walk with God has inspired you. Whoever it is in each category, write down the name, be on the lookout for other examples, and take note of their lives. They may become new role models for you!

Words to Live By

But those who wish to boast should boast in this alone: that they truly know me and understand that I am the LORD who demonstrates unfailing love and who brings justice and righteousness to the earth, and that I delight in these things. —Jeremiah 9:24

POINTER #4 — DIVERSIFY YOUR LIFE

Consider

You've no doubt heard the saying, "Variety is the spice of life!" There is wisdom in this when it is applied to your life and how you spend your time. Are you someone who focuses your life in just a few areas? Or, are your interests varied and your experiences diverse? One way to gauge this is to take a personal diversity survey. Think of the following important areas of life. Rank them from one to twelve in order of their importance to you:

1. Relationships—family and friends
2. Marriage and parenting (down the road)
3. Career (or, in the meantime, school)
4. Spiritual life
5. Entertainment
6. Learning

7. Physical activity
8. Travel and leisure
9. Arts and nature
10. Hobbies
11. Community service/volunteerism
12. Down time

Consider how you're allocating your time to these areas. Is it spread out or concentrated in only a few areas? Now, take your personal inventory: fill in the blank pie chart below according to how you think you're currently allocating your time and energies. What picture emerges and why? While each person is different, variety will diversify who you are and enrich your life!

Example: **Now you try it:**

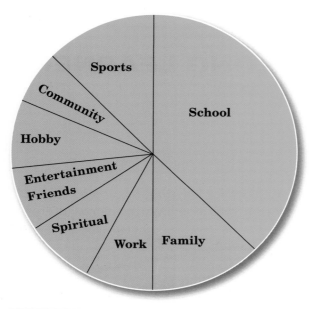

 **Discuss**

Share your pie chart with the rest of the group. Together, brainstorm different opportunities or ideas for expanding experiences and involvement in each of the categories in the list.

 **Apply**

1. This week, talk to your parents about how your family approaches diversifying its lifestyle and how they approach this individually. Ask them to contribute some of their ideas for how you can pursue new interests and activities. Share your ideas and suggestions for a more diversified family lifestyle.
2. Take one idea from your group discussion about diversifying your life and DO IT. Report back to the group what you did and how it impacted you.

Words to Live By

For everything there is a season, a time for every activity under heaven. —Ecclesiastes 3:1

POINTER #5 —
COMMIT TO BEING A LIFELONG LEARNER

Consider

In our global, knowledge-based economy, you need a BIG appetite for learning to succeed. This means not only expanding your career/major subject knowledge, but also having diverse interests. It allows you to explore other subject areas that challenge your mind or satisfy your curiosity. It's also an important asset when meeting new people because you'll present yourself as an interesting person!

Commit to being a lifelong learner. It'll help you advance in your career and make you a more well-rounded and dynamic person. "Joyful is the person who finds wisdom," Proverbs tells us, "and the one who gains understanding" (3:13). Are there subject areas you'd like to explore but haven't—even areas that might be completely different than your career interests? If so, then take the time to identify them and develop a game plan to get started.

List the topics that interest you most (even if you are not currently pursuing or studying them). Think about potential areas such as:

▮ Music and Art

_____

_____

_____

▌ Politics and Government, History

_____

_____

_____

▌ Finances, Investing

_____

_____

_____

▌ Literature

_____

_____

_____

▌ Travel, Culture, Languages

_____

_____

_____

▌ Spiritual Life/Religion

_____

_____

_____

▌ Skills—mechanics, computers, cooking, etc.

_____

_____

_____

▌ Sports—golf, tennis, skiing/snowboarding, team sports, etc.

_____

_____

_____

▌ Outdoors and Nature—hiking, fishing, hunting, rock-climbing, boating/sailing, etc.

_____

_____

_____

Identify some ways you can begin to learn more about these kinds of interests and activities. Consider things like reading, taking lessons, finding a mentor, etc. and develop an action plan.

Discuss

What have you learned lately that did not come from school? How many books, magazines, or newspapers did you read this past year? How many books did you read that were not *required* of you? Have you read your Bible regularly or participated in Bible studies, discipleship, or small groups to help you grow in your spiritual life? Which educational shows, channels, or documentaries have you watched on television (and would you recommend any of them to the rest of the group)? What skills have you learned that someone *showed* you how to do?

Apply

Learn one new thing this week: read something new or watch an educational show. Try a new recipe, explore the library, or visit a museum. Memorize a Scripture verse. Listen to a new style of music or learn a few words of a foreign language. Report back to your group what you learned.

Words to Live By

We ask God to give you complete knowledge of his will and to give you spiritual wisdom and understanding. Then the way you live will always honor and please the Lord, and your lives will produce every kind of good fruit. All the while, you will grow as you learn to know God better and better. —Colossians 1:9–10

Journal

You can use the spaces below to record your thoughts, ideas, and reflections from your personal prayer times as you work through the chapter on "Life Perspective." Your thoughts and ideas, other people's insight and suggestions, things you want to pray about . . . you name it! Whatever you want to write here is just fine—as long as it contributes to helping you develop a sound life perspective and live a life of purpose and impact!

OUTCOMES OF THIS SECTION

After this chapter on "Life Perspective," you should be able to:

▌ Identify some possible components of your life purpose and why you should have one

▌ Be familiar with some of the common life regrets identified by many older people so you can determine NOW to avoid them

▌ Be able to define what success means to you in more than simply monetary terms

▌ Understand what it means to live a diversified lifestyle and take action steps to create balance and variety in your activities and pursuits

▌ Appreciate the value of being a lifelong learner and be intentional about making learning part of your lifestyle

Continue to reflect on the other pointers you read in this chapter of the book, *What I Wish I Knew at 18,* which may not be included in this student manual. The "Take Five" sections are especially helpful to gauge how that particular pointer might be of help or encouragement to you. Don't skip them . . . they may just turn out to be the best part!

Chapter 2 — **CHARACTER**

Demonstrate your capacity to love * ***Cultivate a servant's heart*** * *Be proactively nice* * ***Preserve your reputation and integrity at all costs*** * ***When facing risky situations, ask how your conscience will feel tomorrow*** * ***Stand up for your beliefs and values with conviction*** * *Give everything your best* * *Don't make promises you can't keep* * *Take responsibility for your mistakes and shortfalls* * *Choose humility over self-pride* * ***Solicit and embrace constructive feedback*** * *Laugh often* * *Don't whine . . . just do it!* * ***Be an encourager rather than a critic and always look for the best in people*** * ***Don't say something about someone else that you wouldn't mind them overhearing*** * *Be on "role model behavior" around kids*

> *For though I am far away from you, my heart is with you. And I rejoice that you are living as you should and that your faith in Christ is strong. —Colossians 2:5*

Your character—the moral and ethical fiber of your very being—will have a profound impact on your life. At its core, it's the *who* of who you are. Your character is revealed in vital areas such as your value system, personal standards, temperament, priorities, and relationships with others. Your character is the basic, internal guide to your behavior, and is especially revealed when no one else is looking.

The Bible tells us that no matter how people may appear on the outside, God sees what's really going on inside (1 Samuel 16:7). That means we are always an open book, so to speak, before Him. He cares about our integrity—not because He likes to enforce rules, but because He is a loving Father who is looking out for our best interests. He knows integrity is a protection for us. When we take the high road (make choices that demonstrate godly character), we are protected from many of the unfortunate consequences suffered by those who don't. Integrity definitely has its rewards!

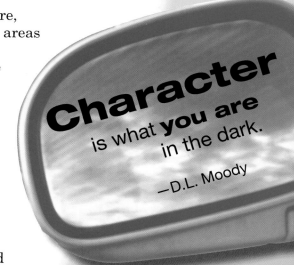

Character is what **you are** in the dark.

—D.L. Moody

Proverbs 2:7
(God) grants a treasure of common sense to the honest. He is a shield to those who walk with integrity.

It's difficult to overstate the importance of your character, and all that flows from it, on how you will ultimately assess your life. In a world that has relaxed some of its values for fear of appearing judgmental, you can take the high road. You can choose to live your life with strong Christian values and be judged by the content of your character. If you do, you'll make the world a better place—and live a life that's overflowing in Kingdom impact.

OBJECTIVES:

▌ Learn the value of prioritizing others over yourself and considering volunteer opportunities to support your community
▌ Become discerning about risky situations and navigate them wisely, protecting your reputation and integrity at all times
▌ Identify your unwavering values and learn to stand up for them when challenged
▌ Intentionally look for the best in other people, and be an encourager rather than a critic to others
▌ Learn to seek out (and receive) constructive feedback and criticism
▌ Challenge yourself to only say things about other people you wouldn't mind them overhearing

Prepare

▌ **Read Chapter Two ("Character") in *What I Wish I Knew at 18*, starting on page 51.**
▌ **Use your highlighter pen to highlight anything in the chapter that jumps out at you—things you want to remember, take note of, come back to, or discuss later.**
▌ **In the chart below, identify the pointers that meet the following criteria:**
   1. the most important in life
   2. ones you think you are already doing well and can model to others
   3. ones you either find the most challenging or in which you may need guidance to apply to your life

1. the most important in life

> **2. ones you think you are already doing well and can model to others**
>
> _____
> _____
> _____
> _____
> _____
> _____
>
> **3. ones you either find the most challenging or in which you may need guidance to apply to your life**
>
> _____
> _____
> _____
> _____
> _____
> _____
> _____

POINTER #1 —
CULTIVATE A SERVANT'S HEART

 Consider

One of the most defining qualities of admired people is their emphasis on others over themselves. Learning to serve others has benefits that far outweigh any sacrifices you'll make and is a source of great joy. Really, our time, talents, and resources are not our own (Psalm 24:1). We are only stewards of all He has given us, and it gives Him (and us!) a great deal of satisfaction when we use it to serve others.

"Serving" can look different in different situations. It can happen on a one-on-one basis—like befriending someone who's not in the inner circle or mowing a lawn for a sick neighbor; in a corporate setting—like sending a birthday card

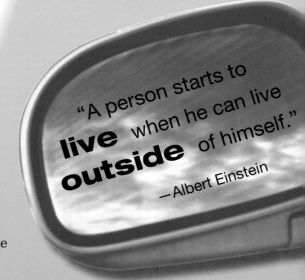

"A person starts to **live** when he can live **outside** of himself."

—Albert Einstein

to a valued client or taking your assistant out to lunch just to express your appreciation; or on a community level—like giving time to a charitable organization or cause. What all of these actions have in common is placing other people's needs above your own interests. Sometimes the only person who will see you do it is God. But that's enough. In fact, Jesus said that when we serve other people with kindness and compassion, it's as if we are serving Jesus Himself (see Matthew 25:35–40)! And, what's not to love about that?!?

Here are some good reasons you should learn to cultivate a servant's heart and volunteer some of your time and energy to serving others: [2]

▮ Experience the intrinsic value and joy of helping others without expecting anything in return.
▮ Connect with your community.
▮ Share your skills and gain new ones.
▮ Develop self-esteem and self-confidence.
▮ Meet new people from all walks of life.
▮ Enhance your resume and make important networking contacts.
▮ Experience new challenges and use your talents in new ways.
▮ Count your blessings while helping people in great need.

There are many different avenues by which you can serve others. Some do it through their *careers*—social workers, teachers, medical practitioners, and clergy quickly come to mind. Still others approach it through *volunteering* their time to a worthy cause. If you go this route, there are three main questions to consider:

▮ What talents and skills do I have to offer?
▮ What groups or community segments (e.g., youth, elderly, homeless) do I feel most called to help?
▮ What organizations will allow me to use my talents to help those I feel most passionately about?

 Discuss

In your small group, discuss the following questions (some may include activities to do together). Be honest and respect others' responses. There are no right or wrong answers and your group should be a safe place to talk and share freely.

Talk about volunteering and various experiences that group members have had with serving others. Maybe some have served the poor or participated in short-term mission trips. What impact did these experiences have on you? On the people being served? Did you gain a new perspective and see the value and joy in using your talents in this way? What potential volunteer opportunities do you see yourself pursuing in the future?

Apply

Find a way to serve someone else without being asked. It doesn't need to be a formal volunteer opportunity. Can you do a task for a parent or sibling? Clean up a portion of the school grounds with a group of friends on a Saturday morning? Babysit a neighbor's children for free so the parents can get a break? Come back and tell your group or class what you did. How did it impact you? What kind of response did you get from the person or people you helped?

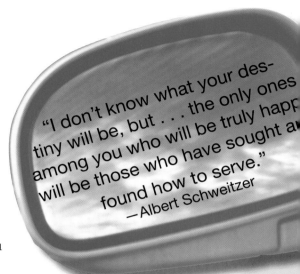

"I don't know what your destiny will be, but . . . the only ones among you who will be truly happ[y] will be those who have sought a[nd] found how to serve."
—Albert Schweitzer

Words to Live By

Don't be selfish; don't try to impress others. Be humble, thinking of others as better than yourselves. Don't look out only for your own interests, but take an interest in others, too. You must have the same attitude that Christ Jesus had. Though he was God, he did not think of equality with God as something to cling to. Instead, he gave up his divine privileges; he took the humble position of a slave.
—Philippians 2:3–7

POINTER #2 —
WHEN FACING RISKY SITUATIONS, PRESERVE YOUR VALUES, REPUTATION, AND INTEGRITY

Consider

There will be times, especially when you graduate from high school and experience newfound freedom in college or move out on your own, you'll be faced with socially (and morally) risky situations requiring *quick* decisions. In some cases, often involving alcohol, drugs, sex,

The most admired people have strong values and the courage to defend them when challenged.

and cheating, these situations may compromise your value system and potentially do irreparable harm to yourself and others. They can be a train wreck that will derail your plans and dreams if you're not careful. During these situations, it's wise to pause and ask how your conscience will feel tomorrow if you answer "yes" or "no"—and what the ramifications of your decision could be to your reputation and integrity.

rep·u·ta·tion

noun \re-pyə-tā-shən\
1 *a* : overall quality or character as seen or judged by people in general *b* : recognition by other people of some characteristic or ability <has the *reputation* of being clever>
2: a place in public esteem or regard : good name <trying to protect his *reputation*>
— rep·u·ta·tion·al \-shnəl, -shə-nᵊl\ *adjective*

in·teg·ri·ty

noun \in-te-grə-tē\
1: firm <u>adherence</u> to a code of especially moral or artistic values : <u>incorruptibility</u>
2: an unimpaired condition : <u>soundness</u>
3: the quality or state of being complete or undivided : <u>completeness</u>

What do we mean by "risky situations?" And why should you care about your reputation and integrity? There are many decisions you can make right now that can have devastating effects on your overall development and well-being, or that might prevent you from future opportunities, successes, and development. This would include behaviors that could cause immediate physical injury (e.g., fighting), as well as behaviors with cumulative negative effects (e.g., drug use). Making the *wrong* decision in these risky situations can also result in your missing out on the normal activities and milestones of youth—the things your friends are enjoying. For example, engaging in sexual activity can lead to teen pregnancy and can preclude you from graduating from high school, attending college, realizing your career dreams, and from enjoying close friendships and activities with your peers.

Don't risk squandering your dreams and losing your good reputation by succumbing to high-risk behavior and situations. Your best bet is to avoid these situations altogether (and if you can't, to at least decide *in advance* how you will react if and when your values are challenged).

THINK ABOUT THIS!

Do you know what your values *are?* You will no doubt continue to hone them over the course of your life, but it's important to identify what principles you are basing your life upon—and then stick to them at all times. One slip up is all it takes to derail your life.

A value is a belief system, guiding principle, or philosophy that determines your decisions, actions, and behaviors. These internal guiding principles motivate you and show others what is important to you. Your values are like a compass, pointing you in a consistent direction. Living your life (and making your decisions) without identifying and being true to your values makes you like a ship without a compass or rudder. You wouldn't know where you were going or have anything to guide you there!

Following are some examples of values. Use the blank spaces to fill in values you can think of that aren't listed here. Then circle the ones that are MOST important to you.

PERSONAL VALUES	SOCIAL VALUES
Healthy living	Compassion
Spirituality/"God-consciousness"	Justice
Self-discipline	Kindness
Fitness	Forgiveness
Punctuality	Grace
Integrity	Flexibility
Commitment	Hospitality
Trustworthiness	Gentleness
Obedience	Righteousness
Courage	Faith
Purity	Patience
Humility	Generosity
Honesty	Gratitude
Cleanliness	Courage
Sense of fun	Perseverance
Thankfulness	Unconditional love
Loyalty	Contentment
Industriousness	Respect
Financial responsibility	Honor
Modesty	Duty
Reliability	Dignity
_____	_____
_____	_____
_____	_____

Discuss

Have you ever been in a risky situation where you had to make a quick decision that challenged your value system? Did you have the courage to go with your values over the pressure you received from others? Did you care more about pleasing and obeying God than you did about impressing (or fitting in with) others, including your friends? If not, how can you better prepare yourself the next time you face a similar situation? *Remember that life is about learning and recovering from our mistakes.* As a group, identify the values that might be compromised in these risky situations and come up with some strategies for making quick positive decisions:

▌ You are invited to a party where you know there will be alcohol. You really like these people and want to fit in with them but not sure that this is the best way to do it—is it?

▌ You have been dating for six months and he/she is putting pressure on you to be more physically intimate than you are comfortable with (or than what you believe is morally acceptable). You're alone together and no parents will be home anytime soon. You don't want to lose this boyfriend/girlfriend. What do you do?

▌ It's time for finals and you've been working overtime at your job earning extra money to pay for a car that you want to buy before graduation. You know your college hopes are riding on your final GPA. You have a golden opportunity to get the answers to the final exam in your most difficult class. An "A" would guarantee you the GPA you need. Should you cheat, just this once? No one will ever know.

Apply

Write the words "CONSCIENCE," "REPUTATION," and "INTEGRITY" on a piece of paper. Post it somewhere you will see it frequently . . . like on your bathroom mirror, a table beside your bed, or the dashboard of your car. Make the commitment to consider and guard these three things when faced with a risky decision.

Words to Live By

Choose a good reputation over great riches; being held in high esteem is better than silver or gold.
—*Proverbs 22:1*

POINTER #3 —
STAND UP FOR YOUR BELIEFS AND VALUES WITH CONVICTION

 Consider

You haven't come this far in life without experiencing peer pressure—it's a part of life, no matter how old you are! Pressure on your value system can range from what brand of jeans you should wear to whom you should date, how you should deal with sex, drugs, and alcohol, and so on. For many, it's only the beginning. Most of the time it will involve social pressure, and it can be tough to stand firm. However, some of today's colleges can sometimes present a new form of pressure.

> Don't think that once you've left high school, you'll get away from pressure to compromise your values.

Sometimes instructors and professors can slip into the role of *indoctrinators* rather than *educators*. There have been instances of outright hostility, intimidation, and grading bias when students do not conform to their professors' views.

Furthermore, being a *Christian* on a secular college campus can pose even more challenges. At a university, you will be exposed to all kinds of new beliefs and ideas, many of which may sound convincing. Some of those ideas—and the people presenting them—will seriously make you question your faith. You may hear ideas and speakers that vehemently denounce your faith. You will no doubt even encounter people on campus who espouse a hatred of Christians and of God Himself. Your faith and values will be tested. The Bible tells us we're not supposed to be surprised when we're questioned or ridiculed—after all, Jesus, His disciples, and the early church faced the same challenge! Rather than being *surprised*, Scripture says, we're supposed to be *prepared* with a right and respectful response: "Always be prepared to give an answer to everyone who asks you to give the reason for the hope that you have. But do this with gentleness and respect" (1 Peter 3:15).

There will be other arenas in which your faith and values will be challenged. In the workplace, there will also be instances where you'll disagree with your manager or employer regarding a business practice or issue. As with the college professor situation, much may be at stake if you resist because they involve values and others in an authority position.

All of these situations are difficult and need to be treated sensitively and carefully. When facing them, you need to:

▌ Know what your own values and convictions are.
▌ Be confident that you have the right to hold your own opinion.
▌ *Respectfully* and *privately* confront and share your position and concerns with individuals who pressure you.

▌ Stick to your guns even if you have to pay a cost (i.e., lose friends).

Looking back at the list of values on page 25, which ones can you say have been challenged the most up to this point in your life? Circle them. Think about how you reacted when they were challenged. Are you happy with the way you responded? Sometimes you just have to consider the source. Why should you compromise your values and integrity in order to be accepted by someone who may be speaking or acting from ignorance or worse? It's okay to agree to disagree and let it be their loss, not yours!

What do you do when your faith in God is being seriously challenged or even ridiculed? Those situations are bound to arise throughout your lifetime, and it's helpful to know in advance how you can respond respectfully and articulately.

Many Christians think it's enough to have a checklist of pat answers they can rattle off when someone challenges their faith. That might sometimes work in the moment, but it usually isn't enough to meaningfully convey the depth and fullness that a living faith in Jesus Christ can offer.

It's important to remember that one reason God is worthy of our worship is that He's big enough to answer all our (and everyone else's) questions. So we shouldn't be intimidated or defensive when our faith in Him is challenged. You can respond by sharing why you believe in God and why it's important to you to obey Him and follow His son, Jesus. And if you don't know the answers to some of the questions being asked, you can simply honestly say, *"I'm not sure how to answer that; can I get back you?"*

Remember that the Bible says, "A gentle answer deflects anger, but harsh words make tempers flare" (Proverbs 15:1). Above all, remember Whom you are representing!

Words to Live By

Live wisely among those who are not believers, and make the most of every opportunity. Let your conversation be gracious and attractive so that you will have the right response for everyone.
—Colossians 4:5–6

Discuss

1. Tear out or copy page 151 ("Values Descriptors") from the Appendix section of this study guide. Cut on the dotted lines. Each person should arrange their slips of paper in order of priority to him or her. Be prepared to explain to each other which are your top five (in order) in each category, and why. Can you think of—and share with the group—examples of how these values affect your decision-making on a regular basis?

2. Role play—Act out the following scenarios:
   Scenario #1—A college professor ridicules a student's belief in a creator God.
   Scenario #2—Someone has a job as a server in a restaurant. A co-worker urges him or her to pocket tips rather than putting them in the common pool of tips for all the servers to divide at the end of the night, as management requires.
   Scenario #3—Someone who just turned 21 is approached by a friend not yet 21, who asks that person to buy alcohol for the younger friend to take to a party.

Above and Beyond

In the Bible, even the apostle Peter got sucked in by peer pressure! Read the story for yourself in Galatians 2:11–16 and see how his friend (and fellow apostle) Paul called him out on it. How do you think YOU would have reacted in that situation . . . if you were Peter? If you were Paul? In your small group, talk about what that might look like to watch out for each other in the area of standing firm in your faith. Close by praying for each other for strength and courage to stand up for what you know is right.

Apply

Take home the slips of paper you cut out from the back of this manual during the values session and share them with family members. Use this as an opportunity to identify which values are shared values in your family (e.g., cleanliness, punctuality, honesty) and which are more important to you as an individual (e.g., justice, compassion), and discuss them.

   Discussion ideas:

▌ Are there ways that having similar values make you closer as a family or ways that conflicts over values create tension?

▌ Ask your parents and/or siblings to arrange the slips of paper in the order that is most important to *them.* You might be surprised!

▌ How have different family members dealt with situations in which their values and beliefs have been challenged, tested, or questioned? Have they ever been significantly challenged in their faith in God? If so, how—and how did they respond?

Words to Live By

Don't copy the behavior and customs of this world, but let God transform you into a new person by changing the way you think. Then you will learn to know God's will for you, which is good and pleasing and perfect. —Romans 12:2

POINTER #4 —
BE AN ENCOURAGER RATHER THAN A CRITIC AND ALWAYS LOOK FOR THE BEST IN PEOPLE

 Consider

We all have opportunities each day to speak into the lives of other people, whether they ask for it or not. Your choice will be to build up or tear down. You've no doubt witnessed these diametrically opposed approaches in the people you've met. People with low self esteem are notorious for cutting down others as a means of building themselves up. However, if you have a desire to be an honorable leader and bring out the best in others, encouragement is far more effective than criticism and negativity. Generally speaking, people put forth a more inspired effort when they are motivated by someone who cares about them. Simply stated, *people try harder to please someone they like and admire.*

> People try harder to please someone they like and admire.

   Bringing out the best in others means you have to look for positive qualities in people, identify them, and call them out. Sometimes, when what you actually see is a negative quality, that can be a real challenge! But it's always possible if you begin by sharing their positive attributes and coach them in an uplifting and constructive manner rather than harshly. It can be helpful in these situations to pray for grace, humility, discernment, and mutual understanding.

BE AN ENCOURAGING LEADER

You've been assigned to a project by your teacher or professor and you are the team leader. Two of the group members are working productively on their parts of the project but a third is slacking. How can you motivate him/her without being resentful or coming across as overly critical? Here are some suggestions:

a. Confront him/her right away; don't stew about it. Resentment and criticism build over time.

b. Do it privately and in person, or at least over the phone—not in writing.

c. Identify first what he's doing right, or if you can't think of anything, mention a positive characteristic (e.g., "I really appreciate the input you gave at our first meeting. You had some really great ideas.")

d. Then mention the issue you're concerned about. ("It seems like we're not getting the benefit of all your great ideas; is there something that's making it difficult for you?")

e. Present yourself as someone willing to help with a problem, not someone who is complaining or blaming. Help him/her brainstorm positive solutions to the problem.

THE ULTIMATE ENCOURAGER

Barnabas was a man in the Bible who was known for his ability to encourage others. In fact, the name "Barnabas" literally means "son of encouragement!" You can read a little bit about Barnabas in Acts 4:36–37, 9:26–28, and 11:24. Notice that when no one else wanted anything to do with Saul of Tarsus (who would eventually become the apostle Paul), Barnabas was the one who believed in him, took him under his wing, and helped Paul find his place in the Christian community. Eventually, mentions of "Barnabas and Saul/Paul" in the Scripture became "Paul and Barnabas" (Acts 13 and onward) as Paul's gifts and calling emerged and Paul took his place of leadership in the early church. But it was Barnabas the Encourager working alongside him to help make that happen. Never underestimate the power of encouragement on others!

 **Discuss**

Role play the following scenarios with an emphasis on delivering encouragement and bringing out the best in others:

- You are coaching a basketball team and you're down by ten points at half-time in a game against your biggest across-town rivals. You need this victory to advance to the playoffs. Up to this point, the team has obviously been lacking intensity. What would you say to motivate them?
- You're ready to make a group presentation to your class, in which all members need to make a short speech. You will be graded as a group. One of the people on your team is profoundly shy and is saying he (or she) cannot go through with it. What do you say? How would you encourage him/her?
- You are the crew chief in your part-time job at a local fast food restaurant. You need to motivate your crew to be able to keep up with production in the kitchen. The movie just got out at the theater next door, the restaurant is crowded, and the orders are coming in faster than your crew can keep up with demand. Give the speech you would give to your crew to get them to speed it up.
- Your friend wants to ask someone of the opposite gender to a special event, but lacks confidence. How would you encourage him or her?

Apply

Practice looking for the best in people. Make a list of three people you tend to be the most critical of (might be a parent, teacher, sibling, co-worker, or classmate). Think about them objectively. Pray and ask God to show you how *He* sees them. Then come up with three positive character qualities—or things you admire/appreciate—for each of them.

POINTER #5 —
SOLICIT AND EMBRACE CONSTRUCTIVE FEEDBACK

Consider

Let's face it. Most of us love to receive compliments—but criticism? Not so much. Criticism, even if it's constructive, can sometimes make us feel guilty, ashamed, or inadequate. We often become angry or withdrawn when we receive it. We can be defensive. Or, out of hurt, we turn the tables on the people criticizing us, attacking their credibility and maybe even their character.

If we're *genuinely* interested in improving ourselves, we should be just as interested in hearing about our weaknesses as we are our strengths—even if the method of delivery is not as kind and gentle as we'd like.

It's a great idea to make it a practice to *actively solicit* constructive feedback from your superiors, friends, and role models. This means asking them questions such as:

> "I like criticism. It's the only way to **grow**."
> —Helen Hayes

▌ Am I meeting your expectations for my performance?
▌ What can I do better?
▌ What do you see are my strengths and weaknesses?

It also means being able to *receive* the feedback you receive, whether you asked for it or not. It's natural to want to be defensive when someone gives you negative feedback—or what feels like negative feedback. But if you do, you'll miss a golden opportunity to learn and grow. Here is some advice for being able to receive criticism well and use it to your advantage:

1. Don't take it personally. If someone criticizes you for something you've done, it doesn't mean they don't *like you*. Learn to separate yourself from the criticism and take it at face value. Think of it as a gift from someone who cares about you!

2. Keep your focus on the feedback, not the people giving it. Don't criticize them in return, or question their credibility, character, or motive.
3. Resist the temptation to interrupt or argue. Thank the person giving you feedback, and assure him or her you'll take it to heart and consider it.
4. Identify what is of value in the criticism, even if you didn't like the way the message itself was delivered. Ask for specifics. Note whether or not this is the first time you've heard this feedback. If so, you may want to give it extra credence.
5. Thank the person for the feedback. If it seems appropriate, enlist his or her help for making changes related to the advice given.
6. Ask for specific examples of any behaviors needing improvement.

 Discuss

Give everyone in your group the opportunity to respond to one or more of the following questions:

1. How do you tend to react when someone criticizes you?
2. Name one current situation in which you would really like to know the "status" of how another person thinks you're doing (for example, a particular class or teacher? A job situation? A sports team on which you're playing?).
3. What do you think is the most important thing to remember when *giving* constructive feedback to someone else?
4. What do you think is the most important thing to remember when *receiving* it?

 **Apply**

Make it a point to ask for one piece of constructive feedback from someone in your life who is a person of influence (such as a parent, teacher, coach, pastor or youth group leader, etc.). Practice responding in the ways you learned about in this section. Record what you learned about yourself in the journal section at the end of this lesson, and how you plan to use the information.

Above and Beyond

In your own prayer time with God, ask Him to give you "constructive feedback" about yourself. David did this when he prayed, "Search me, O God, and know my heart; test me and know my anxious thoughts. *Point out anything in me that offends you*, and lead me along the path of everlasting life" (Psalm 139:23–24, emphasis added).

God's feedback may come through another person's observations (or even criticism), or in a flash of inspiration when you least expect it. Be on the lookout for it . . . and ready to receive it and apply it when it comes!

POINTER #6 —
DON'T SAY SOMETHING ABOUT SOMEONE ELSE THAT YOU'D REGRET IF THEY HEARD

Consider

Words have incredible power. They can be uplifting or destructive. They can be true or false. They can stay solely with the person with whom you've communicated or go in a million different directions outside of your control. This is especially true if you express them in an email, Facebook®, Twitter®, or text. Words also reveal much about our character—especially when we talk about someone who is not present. They speak to our trustworthiness, loyalty, kindness, and respect.

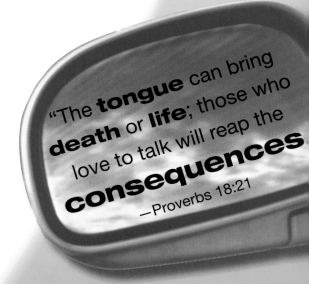

"The **tongue** can bring **death** or **life**; those who love to talk will reap the **consequences**
—Proverbs 18:21

In the past few years, some horrifying tragedies have occurred among young people when unkind things were said either through gossip or on social media sites. Some of these even resulted in suicide. So much heartache— all caused by the power of words.

One way to demonstrate impeccable character is to only say things about other people that you wouldn't mind them overhearing. Try it even for a week and you'll be amazed by how this affects your choice of words. You'll also be admired by others for your tact and restraint.

Discuss

Have you heard about tragedies that occurred because of what people said about other people, either by gossip or on social media? Do these kinds of situations occur in your school or community? Have group members ever had anyone say something negative about them that they found out about later and were shocked, surprised, or hurt by? As a group, come up with some creative ideas for creating a positive culture in your classroom, school, or community. What should you do when you see public criticisms or rumors expressed in social media?

One way to demonstrate impeccable character is to only say things about other people that you wouldn't mind them overhearing.

Apply

1. Do you need to clean up your act when it comes to social media? If you have a social media page, go through it and consider the tone. Is it positive or negative? Are there any posts or photos you need to remove? What would a prospective employer think? They're looking!
2. Think about the tone and content of the words that come out of your mouth. Do they bring "life" or "death" (Proverbs 18:21)? Is there anyone you need to ask forgiveness of for ways you've spoken to or about them? Take the challenge of only saying things you wouldn't mind others hearing—try it for a day, then a week. See how it impacts your thoughts and words.

Journal

You can use the spaces below to record your thoughts, ideas, and reflections from your personal prayer times as you work through the section on "Character." Random thoughts, other people's suggestions, ideas, meaningful Scripture verses or reflections from personal prayer times . . . you name it! Whatever you want to write here is just fine—as long as it contributes to helping you along in your life journey in some way.

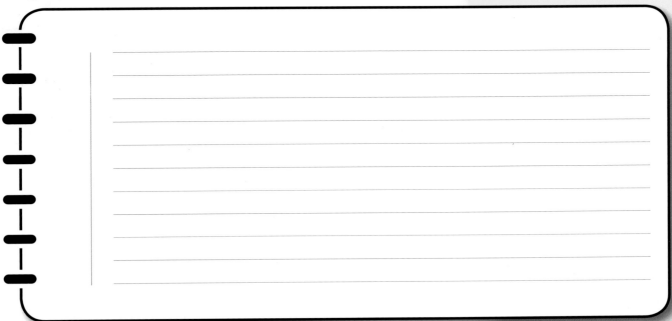

OUTCOMES OF THIS SECTION

After this section on "Character," you should be able to:

- State the value and benefits of serving and identify some ways you can volunteer in your community
- Recognize a "risky situation" and know what steps you can take to either avoid or protect yourself in them
- Define the values you will abide by in your life
- Understand the importance of protecting your reputation and integrity
- Know how (and why) you can best motivate individuals and/or groups of people by encouragement rather than criticism
- Learn to receive feedback and criticism graciously and productively
- Recognize the importance of guarding your words, both verbal and written

Continue to reflect on the other pointers you read in this chapter of the book, *What I Wish I Knew at 18,* which may not be included in this student manual. The "Take Five" sections are especially helpful to gauge how that particular pointer might be of help or encouragement to you. Don't skip them . . . they may just turn out to be the best part!

Chapter 3 — RELATIONSHIPS AND COMMUNICATION

Put relationships before things * *Express yourself* * *Get connected with others who share your interests and values* * *Steer clear of destructive people* * *First impressions are huge* * *Know your audience* * *Be inquisitive when meeting others* * *Enthusiasm is contagious* * *Smile . . . your countenance matters!* * *Notice how others react to you* * *How you say it can matter more than what you say* * *Talk it out, don't write it out* * *Be an inspiring team player* * *Regularly show appreciation and gratitude toward others* * *Strive to be an "agreeable disagreer"* * *Choose reconciliation over grudges whenever possible*

> *Whoever loves a pure heart and gracious speech will have the king as a friend.*
> —*Proverbs 22:11*

Up until now, your relational community has largely consisted of your family, neighborhood, church, and school, and you've probably cultivated your strongest friendships over the course of many years. However, soon many of your lifelong friends will scatter to the four winds to realize their dreams. Some will remain close friends while others will fade away.

At the same time, you'll be offered many opportunities to build new and deeper relationships than you've experienced to date. Whether you enter college or the workforce, you'll be in an amazing atmosphere to make new friends . . . each one starting from scratch! In this process, your ability to cultivate new relationships—and maintain existing ones—will become a vitally important skill to master.

An essential ingredient to healthy relationships is effective communication. How we communicate our ideas, thoughts, and feelings strongly influences the quality of our relationships and our ability to work well with others. In this section, you'll learn some useful pointers for building and maintaining deep and enduring relationships, communicating well, and being regarded by others as a great team player. Your life will be immeasurably richer and your impact far greater when you become a pro at building and sustaining relationships!

OBJECTIVES:

- Learn the value of prioritizing people over things in your life
- Commit to connecting with other people who share similar interests and values, and to steering clear of those who would have a negative influence
- Learn the importance of, and techniques for, making a great first impression
- Demonstrate a curious mindset when meeting new people and be observant to how others react to you

▌ Learn effective communication methods and know when best to communicate by talking versus writing

▌ Seek opportunities to express gratitude and appreciation toward others

Prepare

▌ **Read Chapter Three ("Relationships and Communication") in *What I Wish I Knew at 18*, starting on page 73.**

▌ **Use your highlighter pen to highlight anything in the chapter that jumps out at you—things you want to remember, take note of, come back to, or discuss later.**

▌ **In the chart below, identify the pointers that meet the following criteria:**

1. the most important in life
2. ones you think you are already doing well and can model to others
3. ones you either find the most challenging or in which you may need guidance to apply to your life

1. the most important in life

2. ones you think you are already doing well and can model to others

3. ones you either find the most challenging or in which you may need guidance to apply to your life

POINTER #1 —
PUT RELATIONSHIPS BEFORE THINGS

 Consider

You live in a world that has a lot to offer—and a great deal to distract you from your goals and priorities! On one hand, there are people and relationships, including your relationship with God. On the other hand are other pursuits, like career, wealth, success, possessions, and so on. It's not

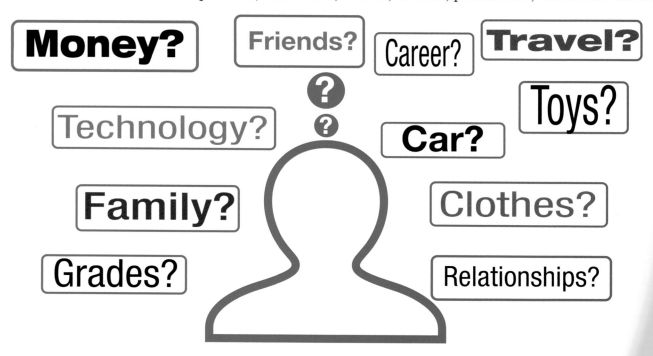

that any of those things are bad in and of themselves—but when pursuing them takes over your life, it can starve your relationships and distract you from what God has called you to do and be. And anyone who's lived long enough can tell you, it's not worth it.

In the last fifty years or so, our society has experienced a marked cultural shift toward accumulating *things,* rather than emphasizing *relationships.* We allow our possessions to define our worth and it's led to widespread financial disasters when people overspend or work 24-7. Contrary to the popular song by Madonna, there is no inherent virtue in being "material."

It shouldn't come as a surprise that, as our society became more consumer-driven, a relationship crisis began to emerge, as evidenced by much higher divorce rates. Too many are over-allocating their time to their careers or accomplishments at the expense of their relationships.

You can start now to be the kind of person that values people over things, money, or power. To accomplish this, one key word to remember is BALANCE.

You've likely encountered people who tried to "do it all" and over-extended themselves. The reality is that no one can do it all (or certainly do it well!). We all have to find that place of equilibrium that gives proper allocation of time, attention, and energy to:

Family
Friends
Career goals
Financial goals
Personal and spiritual growth and fulfillment

Another key word to remember is INTENTIONALITY. Proper balance doesn't just happen by accident. Without a clear plan and commitment to maintaining balance, your allocation to "people priorities" can quickly evaporate. Don't give relationships the leftovers.

 **Discuss**

In your small group, discuss questions or complete the activities in each "Discuss" section. Be honest and respect others' responses. There are no right or wrong answers and your group should be a safe place to talk and share freely.

Give everyone in your group a chance to respond. Compare your answers—which ones are similar? Which are markedly different from person to person?

Read Matthew 6:24–34 as a group. Together, make a bulleted list of the main points Jesus made about priorities. Then discuss the following: Have you ever thought about what you *really* value in life? What are your "must haves?" Take a moment right now to reflect on these questions and record your thoughts. Next, imagine yourself ten years in the future when you have a career, spouse, and family. How might your answers change? How might Jesus' perspective in Matthew 6 influence your response?

_____
_____
_____
_____
_____
_____
_____
_____
_____
_____
_____

 **Apply**

"A Balanced Life" Exercise

This exercise is commonly called a "life wheel" and is frequently used by life coaches.

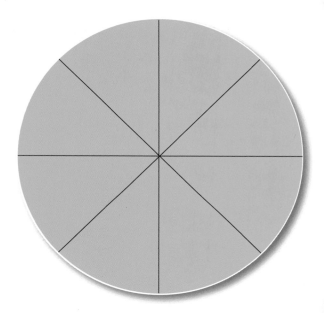

1. Label each section of the circle with an area of your life that is important to you. Examples might include family, friends, health, school, work, recreation/sports, hobbies, money, personal growth, spiritual life, serving/volunteering, dating, etc.
2. In each section, place a dot that represents your level of satisfaction with how much time and energy you are devoting to that area of your life. The outer edge of the circle should represent being "totally satisfied," and the center of the circle should represent being "totally dissatisfied."
3. After placing a dot in the appropriate spot in each pie-shaped section, connect the dots. The line you draw will create a new outside edge to your life wheel. Now evaluate: if your circle were a real wheel and you stood it on edge, would it roll smoothly or not? Which areas need an adjustment?

Words to Live By

Don't store up treasures here on earth, where moths eat them and rust destroys them, and where thieves break in and steal. Store your treasures in heaven, where moths and rust cannot destroy, and thieves do not break in and steal. Wherever your treasure is, there the desires of your heart will also be. —Matthew 6:19–21

POINTER #2 —
GET CONNECTED WITH OTHERS WHO SHARE YOUR INTERESTS/VALUES AND STEER CLEAR OF DESTRUCTIVE PEOPLE

Consider

We all know how intimidating it is to be a new face in a new environment. Most people avoid those situations like the plague! But it's a reality of life that you'll face this challenge over and over. It might be when you go off to college or the military. It might be when you start a new job, move into a new apartment or neighborhood, visit a new church for the first time, or sign up for a fitness club. It might be when you are invited to a party where you won't know many attendees. It's different for everyone, but one goal will be the same—assessing who has the potential to play a part in your life.

With all that in mind, it's important to cultivate new friendships with like-minded individuals who share your interests and values. Don't make the mistake of getting sucked into destructive relationships with negative people because you were so desperate for companionship. Hold on to your identity—and your values!

So how—and where—can you make those kinds of friends? Here are some ideas:

▌ Be self-aware of your own passions, interests, and values.
▌ Identify particular causes or organizations that you're especially passionate about.
▌ Know what hobbies, subjects, and pursuits you enjoy, and how you like to spend your free time.
▌ Recognize the character traits and values you hold most dear and will guard at all costs.

Once you identify the answers, look for opportunities to further those interests and consider where you may find other like-minded people. Whether or not the people you meet *actually share* your interests and values can only be determined by trial and error—but at least you've put yourself in the right spot to find them! Go slowly, ask questions, and spend exploratory time with people. As their interests and values emerge, you'll quickly find out if they are worth spending more time with and could become a long-term friend. **Remember, when it comes to friendships, quality always beats quantity and patience is a virtue!**

If patterns and behaviors indicate a poor match and especially if they possess destructive attitudes or actions—steer clear! Here are some clues:

Remember, when it comes to friendships, quality always beats quantity and patience is a virtue!

- They are involved with pornography, cults, or heavy substance abuse.
- They ridicule your positive choices, values, and interests.
- They are highly critical, negative, and disrespectful—seeing the worst in people
- They put pressure on you to enter their world despite your refusals. They use the "everyone does it" argument.
- They exhibit anti-social tendencies.
- They talk like Christians, but don't "walk the talk."
- They "bring you down," just making you generally feel melancholy, discouraged, and/or depressed.
- They exhibit a lack of motivation or passion for a healthy life.

If you find yourself in a relationship with someone like this, take steps to distance yourself in a big way! Don't get trapped into the feeling that you need to try to help them or fix them. That's not your responsibility. There's a psychology term for toxic relationships like that and it's called *codependency*. It's beyond the scope of this course to address the ramifications of those kinds of relationships, but suffice it to say, you don't want to be in one!

 Discuss

In your small group, talk about times where you have been the new person. How did you get to know people? Was there some trial and error involved before you settled on the friends you did?

Next, come up with two lists together: What are the qualities you look for in good friends? What are the qualities that characterize "not my type?" Reflecting on your acquaintances and friends over the years, what have been the determining factors of whether they became your friend? Have you personally experienced destructive people? What were the signs?

 **Apply**

Following is an exploration of Scriptures that help define honorable relationships. Look up the verses below and note what each says about friendship. You can record your findings in the space provided. Answers are on page 170 in the Appendix.

SCRIPTURE	FRIENDSHIP PRINCIPLE
1 Samuel 18:1–3	
Proverbs 12:26	
Proverbs 16:28	
Proverbs 17:17	
Proverbs 18:24	
Proverbs 20:6	
Proverbs 22:11	
Proverbs 22:24–25	
Proverbs 27:5–6	
Proverbs 27:9	
Proverbs 27:17	
Ecclesiastes 4:9–12	
John 15:13–15	
Proverbs 3:32	
Romans 5:10	
1 Corinthians 15:33	
James 4:4	

POINTER #3 —
RECOGNIZE THAT FIRST IMPRESSIONS ARE HUGE, BE INQUISITIVE WHEN MEETING OTHERS, AND NOTICE HOW OTHERS REACT TO YOU

 Consider

First Impressions Are Huge

There's a wise saying that goes, "You never get a second chance to make a good first impression." Most employment recruiters say that the first 30 seconds of an interview will make or break your chances at the job. Yes, that's *30 seconds*!

Unfortunately, too many people lack the confidence and social skills to make a great first impression. Even very confident people can err on the side of coming across as *too* confident and end up making a negative impression. It's important to just relax, be yourself, and behave with a balance of confidence and restraint.

"You never get a second chance to make a good first impression."

How can you make a great impression? Here's all it takes:

▌ Demonstrate through words *and* body language that you're happy to meet the other person.
▌ Give a firm, confident handshake and look them in the eye.
▌ Smile and be positive and enthusiastic.
▌ Be inquisitive. Show an interest in them and in what they say. Focus more on listening than talking.
▌ Remain engaged in the conversation and avoid distractions like calls and texts.
▌ Be confident but humble and demonstrate good manners.

Be Inquisitive When Meeting Others

"What if I don't know what to talk about?"

This is one of the most frequently asked questions from people who aren't comfortable with carrying on a conversation with someone they've never met before, or whom they don't know well. Here's the secret: You don't have to talk much . . . you just need to learn to ask really great questions, and let the other party do most of the talking! Soon you'll be in the flow of the conversation and they'll be asking you easy-to-answer questions. And, you're off!

Most people love to talk about themselves so put the pressure on *them*. Just make eye contact and show you're interested in what they're saying. Sometimes it helps to write out (or make a mental list) of questions you can ask to be inquisitive and get others talking. You can ask things like:

- "What do you think of ___?" (insert the current situation)
- "How did you get connected/involved with ___?" (insert current situation)
- "Have you been following any sports lately? What are your favorite teams?"
- "How do you know so-and-so?" (maybe referring to the host of the gathering or the person who brought them)
- "How do you like to spend your free time?"
- "What are your plans for this summer?"
- "Are you in school right now or working?"
- "Are you a native of this area? Where are you from originally?"

> Ask a few good questions and be a responsive listener, and people will walk away thinking they made a great new friend in you!

Ask a few good questions and be a responsive listener, and people will walk away thinking they made a great new friend in you! Each question will lead to another and away you go! Finally, it pays to avoid controversial subjects like politics at this stage. Keep it light, keep it fun, and enjoy the adventure of seeing whether today's acquaintance becomes tomorrow's friend!

Notice How Others React to You

You also need to observe how you're coming across to others. Some people are oblivious to the impression they make on others and you don't want to be one of them.

Learn to watch for cues about how others are responding to you. It will show through in their body language, facial expressions, and degree of engagement with you. Do they seem bored? Defensive? Annoyed? Amused? Don't just talk like a machine gun without stopping to check where (and how) your shots are landing. Be in tune with how the other person is reacting to you. If you've lost your audience, sometimes the best thing to do is ask a question and let the other person take over, change the subject, or excuse yourself from the conversation and make a graceful exit.

Here are some self-evaluation questions to help you communicate your best:

- What's my tone of voice? (loud, soft, urgent, shy, aggressive, whiny)
- What's my facial expression? (angry, uncertain, bored, confident, hurt)
- What's my body language? (intimidating, compassionate, encouraging, disinterested, defensive, confident)

In addition to your words, your tone of voice, facial expressions, and body language all contribute to communicating with others. Make it a point to excel in each respect.

Divide into groups of two. Each pair should perform one or both of these role playing exercises for the rest of the group.

Scenario #1

A young job applicant is being introduced to a store manager or business leader. (One person is the applicant, one person is the manager/leader.) The manager should conduct himself as if he or she is a person of some success and authority. The applicant should sincerely behave as if he or she is actually meeting a person in this position. Then:

1. Introduce yourselves (doesn't matter who goes first).
2. Applicant should tell about himself, and ask questions of the manager/leader in an attempt to learn more about him, the company, and the manager's role/position.
3. The manager/leader should inquire of the applicant, find out his interests and skills, and encourage him to tell about himself.
4. Afterward, the person who played the role of manager/leader should give feedback to the person playing the role of the applicant about what kind of an impression he made. The feedback can include: How did the applicant present himself overall? How was the body language and tone of voice? Would the manager be inclined to hire this person based on how he conducted himself?
5. If time allows, take turns and reverse roles so everyone gets the chance to play both parts.

Scenario #2

A new college freshman arrives at a social gathering where he doesn't know anyone. The person he came with has disappeared momentarily, and he is standing alone. There are two friends nearby (sophomores) who know each other well and seem to know everyone else too (at the gathering and on campus).

1. The freshman takes the initiative and says hello. (For a twist, have the two friends initiate and say hello first). Make an effort to "break the ice" (start a conversation).
2. The freshman asks questions of the friends about themselves, what they do, and how to get connected on campus.
3. The friends ask questions of the freshman to get a feel for who he is.
4. Give one another feedback on how each person presented himself and communicated. The feedback can include: How did the

person present himself overall? How was the body language and tone of voice? What did you like about how the person communicated? What could use improvement? (Note: any criticism should be constructive and positively presented.)

 **Apply**

1. Be a people watcher. Observe other people in conversations. Can you see how they are reacting to each other? Watch facial expressions, body language, and tone of voice. What are people saying without using words? What kind of impression are they making? What can you learn about what you observe in other people that you can apply to your own interactions?
2. This one is more specific and personal: Observe people you *know personally* who are unusually good at making new friends. What do they do particularly well that you might be able to include in your own repertoire?

POINTER #4 —
HOW YOU SAY IT CAN MATTER MORE THAN WHAT YOU SAY/TALK IT OUT, DON'T WRITE IT OUT

 Consider

Have you ever found yourself saying, "But, I didn't mean it that way!"? No doubt we all have. But while we can never guarantee how our communication is received by others, we can take steps to ensure we're doing all we can to get our message across accurately.

Believe it or not, research suggests that a whopping 93% of our communication is non-verbal. Of that percentage, approximately 55% percent of what we "say" is our body language, and 38% is our tone of voice—and only 7% of what we communicate is verbal.

It's helpful, then, to be intentional about how we communicate. To that end, there are at least four things that affect how our messages are received by others . . . and any one of them can be the cause of *major* misunderstandings if we're not careful:

1. Consider the *choice of words* and how accurately they convey the intended message.
2. Keep in mind how the words are delivered through *tone of voice, facial expressions, and body language.*
3. Choose carefully the *form* of the communication—verbal or written (which is appropriate for the situation at hand?).

4. Think about the *filter* that may be applied by your audience when they listen to you (unfortunately you can't control it).

Discuss

Make a list of adjectives that describe possible responses to another person's conversation (bored, engaged, angry, amused, etc.) and write them on separate slips of paper. Group members should randomly draw an adjective and act out that attitude or response while the another person does the talking (around 45-50 seconds or so). The talker has to guess the adjective the responder is demonstrating. The purpose of this exercise is to see how well you can detect from another's body language how well you are being perceived—or not!

Apply

Think about this pointer in reverse. How do you react when others communicate about sensitive subjects with you? How do you feel when you receive written communication that you think should have been best handled more personally? Do you give others the benefit of the doubt or are you quick to prejudge what you *think* they're saying? Remember that the tips above work the other way around too!

Words to Live By

A gentle answer deflects anger, but harsh words make tempers flare. —Proverbs 18:1

POINTER #5 —
REGULARLY SHOW APPRECIATION AND GRATITUDE TO OTHERS

 Consider

One of the most uplifting things we experience is when someone expresses appreciation for us, whether as a simple compliment or a thank you for a job well done. Knowing this, we can be a regular "uplifter" to others if we return the favor. It's a win-win for everyone!

Consider the following proven benefits of thankfulness:

- Just 15 minutes a day focusing on the things you're grateful for will boost your body's antibodies (strengthened immune system).
- Grateful people are more focused mentally and measurably less vulnerable to clinical depression.
- Gratitude induces a physiological state of mind called *resonance,* associated with healthier blood pressure and heart rate.

These statistics confirm what God's Word has told us for centuries: "Don't worry about anything; instead, pray about everything. Tell God what you need, and thank Him for all He has done. Then you will experience God's peace, which exceeds anything we can understand. His peace will guard your hearts and minds as you live in Christ Jesus" (Philippians 4:6–7). Being thankful is not just for the benefit of others—it's also good for you!

By regularly showing appreciation and gratitude, your outlook will become more positive and you'll be much more fun to be around.

Do you consider yourself to be a grateful person? Gratitude is the simple attitude (and act) of showing appreciation and thankfulness to God and to other people. It can involve things they have done or appreciation for who they are. It doesn't take a lot of our time or effort to be thankful, but it holds incredible benefits both for the person expressing it and the person (or people) receiving it.

When you're grateful, you focus your mind on pleasant, positive thoughts. It helps you appreciate the things that are happening around you. It prevents you from developing an "entitlement" mindset (the feeling that everyone owes you something). It also raises your happiness quotient!

By regularly showing appreciation and gratitude, your outlook will become more positive and you'll be much more fun to be around. After all, who wants to be around a complainer? Thankful people make the people around them happier too, and ultimately attract more friends and opportunities as a result. Commit to being one!

 **Discuss**

"Thanksgiving" is not just supposed to be for rituals and holidays. God wants it to be our lifestyle! Consider the following passage and discuss the questions below in your small group:

1 Thessalonians 5:16–18
Always be joyful. Never stop praying. <u>*Be thankful in all circumstances,*</u> *for this is God's will for you who belong to Christ Jesus* (emphasis added).

1. What do you think it might look like to be thankful in ALL circumstances, even when you're enduring tough times?
2. Share some times when you felt appreciated by other people. How did they express their gratitude to you? Then brainstorm together some ways you can express gratitude (and to whom). What are some creative ways you can say "thank you" to the people to whom (or for whom) you're thankful? If time allows, each small group should share some of its thoughts with the rest of the class.

 **Apply**

Idea #1: Start a gratitude journal, using the Journal space on the next page, if you like. Each week, jot down some of the things for which you are grateful. You'll be surprised how quickly your list grows—and how positive it makes you feel about your life and the people around you. When you're feeling down, take it out and read it. It'll be sure to lift your spirits.

Idea #2: Commit to expressing gratitude or thanks at least three times a day to others. Carefully observe their response and how you felt delivering it.

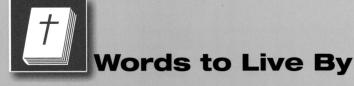 **Words to Live By**

And let the peace that comes from Christ rule in your hearts. For as members of one body you are called to live in peace. And always be thankful. —Colossians 3:18

Journal

You can use the spaces below to record your thoughts, ideas, and reflections from your personal prayer times as you work through the section on "Relationships and Communication."

OUTCOMES OF THIS SECTION

After this section on "Relationships and Communication," you should be able to:

▌ Recognize the value of prioritizing people and relationships over tasks and things

▌ Discover how to connect with positive, like-minded people and how to identify and avoid people who will drag you down

▌ Understand why first impressions are so important and learn how to make a great one

▌ Learn how to get to know people by being inquisitive when you meet them and watching how they react to you

▌ Be conscious that how you say things is as important as what you say

▌ Be more regular and intentional in expressing appreciation and gratitude

Continue to reflect on the other pointers you read in this chapter of the book, *What I Wish I Knew at 18,* which may not be included in this student manual. The "Take Five" sections are especially helpful to gauge how that particular pointer might be of help or encouragement to you. Don't skip them . . . they may just turn out to be the best part!

Chapter 4 — MISCELLANEOUS (BUT IMPORTANT!) LIFE SKILLS

Set and periodically assess your goals * Plan, don't procrastinate * *Time is precious . . . use it wisely* * *Become a masterful decision maker* * Celebrate your victories and learn from your defeats * *Don't let technology control your life* * *Learn to speak comfortably in groups* * *Be a discerning skeptic of all you read and hear* * Drive defensively

This chapter is a collection of success pointers that don't fall neatly into any of the other categories. Nonetheless, they're critically important to your personal productivity, image, and perspective. Master them and it will make a difference!

OBJECTIVES:

▮ Learn how to prayerfully set short-term and long-term goals and to periodically assess/adjust them
▮ Become an effective manager of your time
▮ Develop skills for making sound, well-thought out decisions
▮ Understand the potential downsides of technology use
▮ Recognize the value in learning to speak comfortably in groups
▮ Develop discernment in evaluating what you read and hear

 Prepare

▮ **Read Chapter 6 ("Miscellaneous") in** *What I Wish I Knew at 18*, **starting on page 127.**
▮ **Use your highlighter pen to highlight anything in the chapter that jumps out at you—things you want to remember, take note of, come back to, or discuss later.**
▮ **In the chart below, identify the pointers that meet the following criteria:**

1. the most important in life
2. the ones you think you are already doing well and can model to others
3. ones you either find the most challenging or in which you may need guidance to apply to your life

1. the most important in life

_____
_____
_____
_____
_____
_____
_____
_____

2. ones you think you are already doing well and can model to others

_____
_____
_____
_____
_____
_____
_____
_____
_____

3. ones you either find the most challenging or in which you may need guidance to apply to your life

_____
_____
_____
_____
_____
_____
_____
_____
_____
_____

POINTER #1 —
SET AND PERIODICALLY ASSESS YOUR GOALS

 Consider

Several years ago a movie was released by the name of *The Bucket List*. In it, two terminally ill men escape from a cancer ward and travel around the world in order to fulfill a list of things they want to do before they "kick the bucket." Since the movie's release, the term "bucket list" has gained popularity and now commonly refers to a list of all the things a person would like to do in his or her lifetime. Essentially, a "bucket list" is just a list of specific goals. If you've ever made a bucket list, you're already on your way to being a goal-setter!

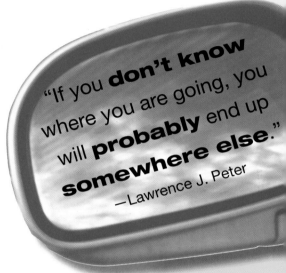

"If you **don't know** where you are going, you will **probably** end up **somewhere else**."
—Lawrence J. Peter

Most successful people begin with dreams and then establish goals and plans to make them come true. The Bible tells us that God has plans for each one of us (Psalm 139:16; Jeremiah 29:11). Our first goal, then, should be to get into alignment with God's heart and plans, and ask for His help in setting our life goals so they match up with His will for our lives. Remember, too, that your goals will materialize and evolve throughout your lifetime, which is okay.

Even if you're not naturally a goal-setter, it's not difficult to become one. Start by imagining what you want your life to look like. What are the large-scale goals you hope to achieve? These are your long-term or *lifetime* goals. It's important to set these first because they will shape your overall perspective and help frame your smaller and shorter-term goals. Think about such areas as:

Most successful people begin with dreams and then establish goals and plans to make them come true.

▌ Education
▌ Career
▌ Marriage and family
▌ Finances
▌ Community service
▌ Physical goals (sports, accomplishments, etc.)
▌ Talents and skills

▌ Travel
▌ Experiences
▌ Retirement

Once you've established your long-term goals, you can set some shorter-term goals (e.g., five years) that will help you achieve your long-term goals. From there, you can set one-year, six-month, and one-month goals, all of which will ultimately contribute to the larger picture.

Periodically check on your long-term goals to make sure they remain high on your list of future accomplishments. Also, monitor your progress on your medium-range goals to make sure you're on track.

Finally, start making daily to-do lists. If you do, you'll be contributing on a daily basis toward the things that will make your lifetime goals and dreams possible. We accomplish so much more when we make to-do lists that reflect our daily goals. People who begin each day with a to-do list know that it makes them much more focused and effective. In fact, the discipline of writing down tasks and the sense of accomplishment received from completing them are qualities of a productive person.

Discuss

In your small group, discuss the following list (some may include activities to do together). Be honest and respect others' responses. There are no right or wrong answers and your group should be a safe place to talk and share freely.

Using the "Bucket List" page provided in the Appendix on page 156, make a list of long-term goals you'd like to accomplish in your lifetime. Compare your lists with one another. Share why you chose the goals you did and what you will have to do to achieve them.

Apply

Take your bucket list and transfer it to page 157 in the Appendix, "Goals." Put the items in the appropriate sections for short-term, medium-term, and long-term goals. Here are some guidelines as you do:

▌ Phrase your goals in the positive, not the negative.
▌ Make them realistic goals—ones that are possible and achievable.
▌ Make them measurable and specific, such as "visit five continents" as opposed to "travel around the world."

Words to Live By

No, dear brothers and sisters, I have not achieved it, but I focus on this one thing: Forgetting the past and looking forward to what lies ahead, I press on to reach the end of the race and receive the heavenly prize for which God, through Christ Jesus, is calling us. —Philippians 3:13–14

Therefore, since we are surrounded by such a huge crowd of witnesses to the life of faith, let us strip off every weight that slows us down, especially the sin that so easily trips us up. And let us run with endurance the race God has set before us. We do this by keeping our eyes on Jesus, the champion who initiates and perfects our faith. —Hebrews 12:1–2

POINTER #2 —
TIME IS PRECIOUS, USE IT WISELY

Consider

You have three primary assets in life—your time, your talent, and your treasure. Because the first of those assets—time—is limited, you need to learn to use it wisely. That means you need to become a good time manager.

How do you become a good manager of time? Consider the following list (excerpted from *What I Wish I Knew at 18*). In the spaces to the left, place a check mark next to the ones you think you are already strong in. Place a question mark next to the ones you think you need to work on.

_____ Treat your time as a precious asset with limited capacity.

_____ Organize a to-do list by urgency (deadline) and priority (importance). Take both into account when deciding what to focus on each day.

_____ "Block" your time (i.e., group it in 30–60 minute intervals *without* interruption) in order to complete your highest priority assignments. Avoid interspersing lower priority tasks within your high priority assignment intervals.

_____ Don't hesitate to politely tell someone that it's an inconvenient time for you. Interruptions can destroy your productivity if you allow it.

_____ Learn to multi-task (i.e., simultaneously perform) your lower priority responsibilities.

_____ Keep your cell phone somewhere else when you need focused time. The temptation to answer calls and texts can be a major distraction.

_____ Take periodic breaks. Studies have shown people are less productive when they work over an hour straight without a five-minute break. Breaks help your mind recharge.

_____ Avoid all-nighters.

_____ Find your best venue for focused work.

_____ Respect and honor others by being punctual. Don't be known for being late and wasting others' time!

 Discuss

Complete the assessment below and share your score with the rest of the group. Talk about why you think you scored the way you did. Help one another brainstorm ways to be better time managers. Some of you may be strong in the areas where others are weak. Pool your strengths and time management strategies.

TIME MANAGEMENT ASSESSMENT

In each statement set below, mark the one that best describes you, and then circle and write the corresponding score in the margin:

_____ 1 I plan ahead for completing major projects/studying for exams and do a little each day.

_____ 2 I wait for the teacher to remind me that something is due soon and then I get cracking.

_____ 3 I wait until the night before a project is due or test is scheduled and cram like crazy.

_____ 1 I _almost always_ complete my school homework and/or daily assignments.

_____ 2 I _usually_ complete my school homework and/or daily assignments.

_____ 3 I often _don't_ complete my school homework and daily assignments, or I turn them in late.

_____ 1 I like to finish assignments and reports with time to spare.

_____ 2 I like to finish assignments and reports exactly on their due dates.

_____ 3 I sometimes finish assignments and reports a little late.

_____ 1 I always have my watch/phone/clock set to precisely the correct time.

_____ 2 I like my watch/clock to be set a few minutes ahead of the correct time.

_____ 3 Most of the time, I don't wear a watch or pay attention to the time on my cell phone.

_____ 1 I tend to arrive at most events and appointments at least five minutes early.

_____ 2 I tend to arrive at most events and appointments exactly on time.

_____ 3 I tend to arrive at most events and appointments a little late.

_____ 1 I tend to walk and talk quite quickly as I go about my daily activities.

_____ 2 I tend to take my time as I go about my daily activities.

_____ 3 I tend to walk and talk quite slowly as I go about my daily activities.

_____ 1 I rarely spend more than 15 minutes at a time talking or texting on my phone.

_____ 2 I sometimes spend more than 15 minutes at a time talking or texting on my phone.

_____ 3 I often spend more than 15 minutes at a time talking or texting on my phone.

_____ 1 I never watch more than 1 ½ hours of TV on a weeknight.

_____ 2 I sometimes watch more than 1 ½ hours of TV on a weeknight.

_____ 3 I usually watch more than 1 ½ hours of TV on a weeknight.

_____ 1 I never spend more than an hour on Facebook® (or other social media) or video games at any one time.

_____ 2 I sometimes spend more than an hour on Facebook® (or other social media) or video games at one time.

_____ 3 I usually spend more than an hour on Facebook® (or other social media) or video games at one time.

Now add up your scores and write the total here _____

The higher the total, the more you need to work on time management skills now. If your total is over 12, you probably need to adjust your priorities and begin to take more responsibility for managing your time. The older you get, the more important this becomes. Sorry, but that's life!

Apply

Start each day with a prioritized to-do list for a week. Afterwards, reflect: How did it change your overall productivity? Order and organizational sense? What did you accomplish that you might have otherwise forgotten? Did you notice the difference?

Above and Beyond

The Bible shows us over and over that God cares about how we spend our time—and will help us use it wisely and for His glory if we let Him. Jesus always spent time in prayer seeking God's direction before going out to minister (Mark 1:35; Luke 6:12–13), as did Paul and the early church leaders (Acts 13:2–4). As you begin making a practice of developing daily or weekly to-do lists, be sure to include prayer as part of the process. Instead of coming up with your own ideas first, start by asking God to help you decide how to spend your time!

Words to Live By

We can make our plans, but the LORD determines our steps. —Proverbs 16:9

POINTER #3 —
BECOME A MASTERFUL DECISION MAKER

Consider

The fact is most of our daily decisions have little consequence. Whether you have spaghetti or chicken for dinner tonight won't mean a hill of beans ten years from now. But what about the college you attend? The career you select? The job offer you take? The person you marry? The number of children you have? These are life-changing decisions that are made with unknown consequences. And what makes them especially challenging is that many are first time decisions, with no prior history to guide us!

Often, people make decisions impulsively and based on emotion rather than on a thorough and objective evaluation accompanied by prayer for God's direction and a sense of the leading of the Holy Spirit. That's where long-term consequences can get serious. Making tough decisions is never easy. However, if you practice the following six steps (more fully explained in *What I Wish I Knew at 18,* page 132–133), your odds of making the right decision the first time will be significantly greater:

Step 1: Get the facts.
Step 2: Determine your key decision criteria.
Step 3: Identify all of your alternatives.
Step 4: Pray and engage wise counsel.
Step 5: Conduct a comprehensive pro/con list of your alternatives.
Step 6: Consider your "gut instinct" or intuition, being sensitive and alert to the Holy Spirit's leading and direction.

Chances are, by the time you've completed the fifth step, your best choice will have emerged. However, the final test is what you believe God's Spirit is telling you. If, after completing steps 1–5, you have a nagging feeling that it isn't right, sleep on it. If you're still uncertain the following day, have a heart-to-heart talk with yourself, God, and your most trusted advisors. This will either reinforce your preliminary decision (which will provide the needed conviction) or it will compel you to more seriously consider your other alternatives.

Discuss

Good decision-making happens by being thorough, objective, rational, prayerful, and after seeking wise counsel—not by some mysterious or mystical process! In your small group, talk about the ways you make decisions, and why. Reflect on decisions you made wisely versus those made erratically. How do you deal with decisions where your mind says one thing but your emotions guide you elsewhere? What have been the hardest decisions you've made in your life? If you have effective strategies, share them with the rest of the group.

Then together, come up with two lists:

- Top five most common decisions high school students have to make on a regular basis (low-impact)
- Top five most stressful decisions high school students WILL LIKELY (or even just possibly) have to make during their college and career years—use your imagination!

TOP FIVE MOST COMMON DECISIONS	TOP FIVE MOST STRESSFUL DECISIONS

If time allows, groups can share their lists with the rest of the class.

Above and Beyond

One of the most delightful privileges of being a child of God is the ability to hear His voice. Throughout Scripture and throughout history, God has consistently demonstrated His love for His people by communicating with them in a variety of ways. For example, He told Jeremiah, "Call to me and I will answer" (Jeremiah 33:3, NIV). "My sheep listen to my voice," said Jesus (John 10:27, NIV). Hearing from God is supposed to be perfectly normal for His children!

    Have you ever asked God for help with a specific decision you had to make, and had a dramatic answer? If so, share it with your group. From here on in, make it a practice to stop before you decide and ask Him to show you what He wants you to do!

Apply

Activity #1 How Good Are Your Decision-Making Skills?[4]

Instructions:

For each statement, mark the circle in the column that most applies. Then add up your score and check your result using the scoring table at the bottom of the next page.[3]

	Statement	Not at all (1)	Rarely (2)	Some-times (3)	Often (4)	Very Often (5)
1	I evaluate the risks associated with each alternative before making a decision.	○	○	○	○	○
2	After I make a decision, it's final—because I know my process is strong.	○	○	○	○	○
3	I try to determine the real issue before starting a decision-making process.	○	○	○	○	○
4	I rely on my own experience to find potential solutions to a problem.	○	○	○	○	○
5	I tend to have a strong "gut instinct" about problems, and I rely on it in decision-making.	○	○	○	○	○
6	I am sometimes surprised by the actual consequences of my decisions.	○	○	○	○	○
7	I use a well-defined process to structure my decisions.	○	○	○	○	○
8	I think that involving many stakeholders to generate solutions can make the process more complicated than it needs to be.	○	○	○	○	○

9	If I have doubts about my decision, I go back and recheck my assumptions and my process.	○	○	○	○	○
10	I take the time needed to choose the best decision-making tool for each specific decision.	○	○	○	○	○
11	I consider a variety of potential solutions before I make my decision.	○	○	○	○	○
12	Before I communicate my decision, I create an implementation plan.	○	○	○	○	○
13	In a group decision-making process, I tend to support my friends' proposals and try to find ways to make them work.	○	○	○	○	○
14	When communicating my decision, I include my rationale and justification.	○	○	○	○	○
15	Some of the options I've chosen have been much more difficult to implement than I had expected.	○	○	○	○	○
16	I prefer to make decisions on my own, and then let other people know what I've decided.	○	○	○	○	○
17	I determine the factors most important to the decision, and then use those factors to evaluate my choices.	○	○	○	○	○
18	I emphasize how confident I am in my decision as a way to gain support for my plans.	○	○	○	○	○

Total = _____

Score Interpretation

Score	Comment
18–42	Your decision-making hasn't fully matured. You aren't objective enough, and you rely too much on luck, instinct or timing to make reliable decisions. Start to improve your decision-making skills by focusing more on the process that leads to the decision, rather than on the decision itself. With a solid process, you can face any decision with confidence.

43–66

Your decision-making process is OK. You have a good understanding of the basics, but now you need to improve your process and be more proactive. Concentrate on finding lots of options and discovering as many risks and consequences as you can. The better your analysis, the better your decision will be in the long term. Focus specifically on the areas where you lost points, and develop a system that will work for you across a wide variety of situations.

67–90

You have an excellent approach to decision-making! You know how to set up the process and generate lots of potential solutions. From there, you analyze the options carefully, and you make the best decisions possible based on what you know. As you gain more and more experience, use that information to evaluate your decisions, and continue to build on your decision-making success. Think about the areas where you lost points, and decide how you can include those areas in your process.

Copyright by MindTools.com and used by citations permission. This assessment activity and many other extraordinary helps may be found on the Mind Tools site at http://www.mindtools.com/pages/article/newTED_79.htm#

 Words to Live By

Trust in the LORD with all your heart; do not depend on your own understanding. Seek his will in all you do, and he will show you which path to take. —Proverbs 3:5–6

POINTER #4 — DON'T LET TECHNOLOGY RULE YOUR LIFE

 Consider

No one would dare argue that this generation is dominated by technology. Young people today have cell phones, computers, video games, iPods, and a host of other electronic devices that entertain them, educate them, and help them communicate. Inarguably, technology has improved our lives in dramatic ways. It has made our work far more efficient and communication more rapid and widespread. We are far more connected, at least on the surface, because of amazing advancements in technology.

But as with any advancements, even technology has its down sides. For example, our world is getting more impersonal as it becomes more technological. We text or email rather than talk. Our lives are more distracted because of our numerous interruptions and our attention spans have shrunk. We are spending less time reflecting and using our imaginations. People are becoming more sedentary. Our waist lines are showing it!

It's all too easy to fall into the trap of relying on electronics to make life happen. But remember that time is a precious asset and that relationships are designed to be *personal*. Don't let your electronic devices interfere with that!

 **Discuss**

Mentally walk through your day. In what ways do you use technology at home, school, work, and elsewhere, all day long? Make a list identifying the different items you use from morning to night. How long is your list? Are you surprised?

 **Apply**

Try to go a full day screen-free. No cell phone, no TV, no computer (except for homework), no video games, etc. Use the time you otherwise would have used on-screen to interact with people like family and friends, face to face. How hard was it for you to do? Record in your journal pages at the end of this section what you did with your time and report back to your group. Who had the most creative ideas for what to do?

POINTER #5 — LEARN TO SPEAK COMFORTABLY IN GROUPS

 Consider

When people are asked to identify their greatest fear, one of the most commonly mentioned is "public speaking in front of an audience." There is even a special name for this common anxiety: *glossophobia!*

The idea of standing in front of people to deliver information or make a persuasive speech is terrifying for millions of people. Giving a public talk, however, does not have to feel like a near-death experience. Speaking comfortably in front of groups is a skill that *can* be learned. Acquiring this skill will help you immensely in life, especially as you advance in your career. Consider these pointers to help you improve:

Speaking comfortably in front of groups is a skill that *can* be learned. Acquiring this skill will help you immensely in life.

- Lower your expectations of yourself—you don't need an orator's eloquence to deliver a successful presentation.
- Realize that you usually know more about your subject than your audience and only you know exactly what you want to say—take comfort in this!
- Recognize and understand that most audiences want you to succeed—they're on your side.
- Avoid excessive detail (especially when it is technically beyond your audience).
- Remember that people love stories.
- Show lots of enthusiasm and expression.
- Occasionally start with a question to the audience—it really settles down your nerves and they like it!
- Understand that butterflies are normal. You might think you're coming off as a nervous wreck, but your audience won't detect minor nervousness at all.
- Seek opportunities to lead a small group of friends—this will give you good practice.

 **Discuss**

Each person in the group should select a topic or starter from the list below. After allowing a short time (like a minute or two) for everyone to gather their thoughts, each person should take a turn standing in front of the rest of the group and speaking on his or her topic for TWO minutes. Use a cell phone or watch as a timer. You can't sit down until you've talked on your topic for two minutes.

HOT TOPICS

What I Enjoy about the Sport of _____

Interesting and Authentic Ways to Share Your Faith

What I Would Do with a Million Dollars and Why

Why We Celebrate Thanksgiving

Why (insert place name) Is a Fabulous Place to Visit/Travel

Should the Homework Load for High School Students Be Officially Limited to Two Hours?

How Should You Choose the Best College for You?

Media Bias and How to Be Discerning of It

My Nickname and How I Got It

If I Were the Teacher, This Class Would Be Different (and How)

The Hardest Thing I've Ever Done

I Am a Famous Athlete!—My Best Moments of the Game

How to Prepare (insert name of meal/dish here)

My favorite holiday memory was . . .

My all-time favorite movie is . . .

My all-time favorite vacation was . . .

My funniest experience was . . .

If I could change one school policy it would be . . .

Why my most likely career choice is . . .

To me, a successful life is . . .

Above and Beyond

Prepare a short devotional message or Bible lesson and share it with the rest of your group. Include Scripture verses, practical application of the principles you are sharing, and personal stories from your own life to illustrate your points.

Apply

Extra practice: Give your speech to someone at home. Was it better the second time you did it? Did you feel more comfortable? What was different? Remember, "practice makes less imperfect!"

POINTER #6 —
BE A DISCERNING SKEPTIC OF ALL YOU READ AND HEAR

Consider

Perhaps there was a time when the news media was more balanced in reporting news and views, but those days are long gone. You can detect it in how news shows and newspapers convey the "facts," as well as in what they choose to report. Increasingly, we see media outlets with a strong political slant completely color the news through their own lens—rather than reserving their opinions for the editorial page. You see it when Christian groups are characterized by the actions of extremists who do not really represent God's heart and character, but who serve some media's purposes of painting Christians as judgmental, extreme, or off base. Media outlets are notorious for conveying bad news over good news—based on studies of viewer behavior.

This trend has not gone unnoticed by the general public. In increasing numbers viewing audiences recognize the media's tilted perspective. A 2005 survey conducted for the *American Journalism Review* found nearly two-thirds of the public disagreed with the statement, "The news media try to report the news without bias."[4]

Because of this pervasive editorial slant, you have to learn to be a discerning skeptic of what you read and hear. How do you deal with this reality? Here are a couple of suggestions for remaining well informed and not being easily misled:

▌ Try to get all sides of an issue.

▌ When it comes to political campaigns, recognize the candidates will tell you what they think you want to hear (they assume you'll forget by the next election!).

▌ When it comes to news outlets, 1) watch different channels with different political tendencies and 2) look at the election endorsements of your newspaper to gauge their political tendencies.

▌ Read the footnotes and caveats in any advertisements or promotions.

▌ Beware of panel discussions on news shows where all agree on a subject—that media outlet is possibly biased.

 **Discuss**

In your small group, appoint one person as the moderator (or discussion leader) and discuss the following questions:

1. How important is the news media's role in a democracy? To what extent are we dependent on the news media for political information? What might be other ways of getting information about politics, issues, and elections?

2. Nearly everyone agrees that news coverage in mainstream news is becoming more negative and entertainment-oriented. Why do you think this has happened and what do you think are the consequences?

3. Identify some subject areas in the news which might be skewed in their presentation because of the editorial slant of either the reporter or network.

4. Statistics indicate that younger viewers are turning away from conventional methods of news reporting. Why do you think this might be? What are some other ways people can stay accurately informed about issues and what's going on in the world?

 **Apply**

Watch the news on several different networks and read several articles in more than one major newspaper (you can look online). Can you find any examples of media bias? Of Christians or Christian principles being mischaracterized? What slant(s) do you see? What kind of bias is it (political, advertising, corporate, mainstream, or sensationalism)? Record your findings in the Journal section and report back to your class what you found.

Words to Live By

And the people of Berea were more open-minded than those in Thessalonica, and they listened eagerly to Paul's message. <u>*They searched the Scriptures day after day to see if Paul and Silas were teaching the truth*</u>*. —Acts 17:11 (emphasis added)*

Journal

You can use the spaces below to record your thoughts, ideas, and reflections from your personal prayer times as you work through the section on "Miscellaneous (but Important!) Life Skills."

OUTCOMES OF THIS SECTION

After this section on "Miscellaneous (but Important!) Life Skills," you should be able to:

- Set short-term and long-term goals and know how to assess/adjust them periodically
- Effectively plan and manage your time
- Have a framework for making sound, well-thought out decisions
- Understand the potential downsides of technology use and be able to go without it from time to time
- Be more comfortable speaking in front of a group
- Be aware of media bias and know how to evaluate what you read and hear

Continue to reflect on the other pointers you read in this chapter of the book, *What I Wish I Knew at 18,* which may not be included in this student manual. The "Take Five" sections are especially helpful to gauge how that particular pointer might be of help or encouragement to you. Don't skip them . . . they may just turn out to be the best part!

Chapter 5 — COLLEGE ACADEMICS

*Excelling is about planning, preparing, and performing * Consider the rainbow highlighter study method*

> *And this I pray, that your love may abound still more and more in real knowledge and all discernment, so that you may approve the things that are excellent, in order to be sincere and blameless . . . —Philippians 1:9–10*

When you graduate from high school, you'll soon find that life will never be the same. And, few areas will change as much as your academic environment if you attend college. The pressure soars along with the competition, and if you don't modify your study habits, your academic success might be a thing of the past. That's the way it started out with me!

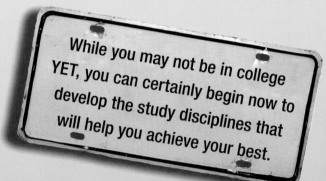

While you may not be in college YET, you can certainly begin now to develop the study disciplines that will help you achieve your best.

Many factors will determine your academic progress after high school, and this chapter can help you along the way. While you may not be in college YET, you can certainly begin now to develop the study disciplines that will help you achieve your best in whatever educational venue you pursue (including job training). And, if you're still in high school, these insights might help give you a GPA boost before taking the next step.

The key point to understand is this: *How you prepare is just as important as your innate intelligence.* That's the secret to the study method you are about to learn, and it has had highly effective results with students who have adopted it.

OBJECTIVES:

▌ Learn to plan, prepare, and perform to achieve your best academic success

▌ Develop a disciplined study routine and method

 **Prepare**

▐ Read Chapter 7 ("College Academics") in *What I Wish I Knew at 18*, starting on page 147.

▐ Use your highlighter pen to highlight anything in the chapter that jumps out at you—things you want to remember, take note of, come back to, or discuss later.

▐ In the chart below, identify the pointers that meet the following criteria:

1. the most important in life
2. ones you think you are already doing well and can model to others
3. ones you either find the most challenging or in which you may need guidance to apply to your life

1. the most important in life

2. ones you think you are already doing well and can model to others

3. ones you either find the most challenging or in which you may need guidance to apply to your life

POINTER #1 —
EXCELLING IS ABOUT PLANNING, PREPARING, AND PERFORMING

 Consider

It's true that there's no such thing as a one-size-fits-all, most-effective-ever study method. You are your own person with your own unique learning capacities and strategies. That being said, there *are* some common themes to excellent study habits. Surprisingly, it doesn't necessarily mean studying MORE. It does mean learning to study SMART! It's all about three key ingredients:

1. Good planning

There are only so many hours in a day, a week, a quarter, or semester. However, while you can't change the number of hours, you *can* decide how to best use them. To be successful in school, you must carefully manage your study time. If you aren't a good planner, you *will* struggle. It's as simple as that.

If you aren't a good planner, you will struggle.

Part of good planning involves being *proactive* rather than *reactive*. Being proactive means you make a habit of being "on it." You do what needs to be done without putting it off or waiting for other people to force you into it. Simply put, it means you assume responsibility and take initiative for your life, rather than waiting and responding to what others do or demand. What this looks like in the context of studying is:

▮ Planning ahead (not procrastinating)
▮ Spreading out your preparation time (not cramming)
▮ Being disciplined (not allowing distractions to sidetrack you)
▮ Prioritizing (not being distracted by things that are less important)
▮ Taking the need to study seriously (not being overconfident)

pro·ac·tive
adj \prō-ak-tiv\
pro- + re*active* : acting in anticipation of future problems, needs, or changes

re·ac·tive
adj \rē-ak-tiv\
1 : of, relating to, or marked by <u>reaction</u> or <u>reactance</u>
2 : readily responsive to a stimulus *b* : occurring as a result of stress or emotional upset

For example, you can learn to be proactive about planning your schedule, ensuring that your time is most effectively spent. That doesn't mean you don't have any down time or fun! It just means you are less likely to *waste* time. And that is enough to make a real difference in your academic performance, as well as other areas of your life.

Note: See the sample weekly planner and daily schedule provided on pages 158 and 159 of this study guide. You may make photocopies of these for your personal use.)

2. Good preparation

Besides learning to plan your schedule, it's essential to develop an effective study *discipline*. That means staying committed to your study schedule, becoming a skilled time manager, being attentive in class and an effective note taker, and finding a study environment that works best for you. Do you have a place to study that is comfortable, well-lit, supplied with everything you need, and can be free of distractions (at least, to the degree that you want it to be)? Are you well-rested and alert? All of these things contribute to being well-prepared for academic excellence.

"The **key** is not to **prioritize** what's on your schedule, but to **schedule** your **priorities**."
—Stephen Covey

3. Great performance

Great performance means delivering what your audience (in this case, your teacher or professor) is looking for. It means entering your exams with supreme confidence that you've planned—and are prepared—to excel. This includes more than just your study habits. Great performance is also linked to:

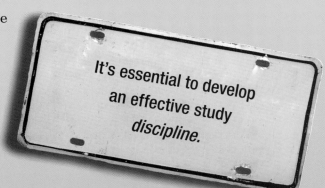

It's essential to develop an effective study discipline.

▌ Regular attendance
▌ Class participation (it pays to sit in the front row!)
▌ Being organized
▌ Finding a balance between academics, social life, and any job or extracurriculars
▌ Taking care of your physical and spiritual health and well-being

 **Discuss**

In your small group, talk about your answers to the following questions (some may include activities for you to do together). Be honest and respect others' responses. There are no right or wrong answers, and your group should be a safe place to talk freely.

1. Are you an organized and disciplined studier? Why or why not?
2. What do you think about the statement, *"Improving study habits doesn't necessarily mean studying MORE; it means learning to study SMART."* Do you agree or disagree?

3. What are some proven ways or methods you have learned to help you study smarter? Share your personal study tips in your group. Use the journal section at the end of this chapter to record any study or testing ideas from other people in your group that you'd like to remember and try out.

 **Apply**

Make copies of the weekly planner and daily schedule supplied on pages 158 and 159 in the Appendix section.

1. If you have syllabi from each of your classes, note the due dates of major tests, projects, and assignments, and transfer them into your weekly calendar as they come up.
2. Each Sunday, before you start the following week, record all known assignments and activities into the appropriate dates on the calendar. Add to them during the week as more assignments and projects come up.
3. Use the daily schedule to plan and block out hours of time to complete assignments and to study.

POINTER #2 —
CONSIDER THE RAINBOW HIGHLIGHTER STUDY METHOD

 Consider

The study method you're about to learn primarily involves test taking and preparation. It tends to be more applicable to courses that are more exam-oriented than papers-oriented. The beauty of it is that it will help you enter exams with supreme confidence which is crucial in high pressure situations. Here are the elements of the approach:

1. Know your audience (your particular teacher or professor).
2. Take detailed notes.
3. Highlight what you read.
4. Complete all reading four days before the test date.

5. Develop your study schedule (including a four-day review period).
6. Review your material using the "rainbow highlighter method."
7. Have a proven test-taking strategy.
8. Analyze your performance and make mid-course adjustments.
9. Ask the teacher for help when necessary.

Here's how the rainbow highlighter method works: As you read your textbook, start with a yellow highlighter and highlight *everything* you feel is important and that you would probably not remember after just one reading. After your first pass, you might have as much as half a page highlighted, but that's okay. Complete all required reading FOUR DAYS BEFORE THE EXAM DATE.

Remember, reps are good for body and mind!

Then, start your review by *rereading the yellow highlighted portion* from your initial reading. Because this will be your second reading, your ability to understand and recall it will be twice as good. However, there still may be details or concepts you might not feel totally confident you'd remember if you took the exam tomorrow. In these places, simply take a different color highlighter (such as lime green), and highlight those sentences where you would like to have yet another review tomorrow.

At this point, your pages have three colors: plain, yellow, and yellow-green. Repeat this process again the next day using yet a different color (such as orange), but only reread the yellow-green section. You're now reading this information for the fourth time, highlighting in orange any sentences you want to read again tomorrow. This will be yet a further reduction in the amount you need to reread.

You can see how your confidence grows and grows as the amount of material you highlight shrinks and shrinks. At the end of the study review period, just prior to the test, you've used several different highlighted colors and seen the most *difficult* material four to five times. This degree of repetition has a powerful impact on your ability to recall the material and on your confidence as you enter the exam. Remember: reps are good for body and mind!

 **Discuss**

Supplies needed: four colors of highlighter pens

1. Practice using the "rainbow highlighter" study method with your small group. Following are two pages from *What I Wish I Knew at 18.* Using the rainbow highlighter method described (and which is illustrated on page 236 of the *What I Wish I Knew at 18* book), study this page together. One person can read aloud while the rest of the group highlights the text. Do this four times, each time using a different color pen and only highlighting sections you're not sure you'll remember. You may need to share pens if there aren't enough to go around. (Obviously, this is an accelerated way of using the study method, for instructional purposes only. Normally you would do it over the course of four days prior to an exam.)
2. Next, take the test on the "Be the Only You" pointer, supplied on page 160 in the Appendix section. Check your answers together as a group. How was your recall of the material?

BE THE ONLY YOU

More often than not, progress is a two steps forward and one step backward proposition. The technological advances of the last two decades are a good case in point. We are so much more efficient and productive and in many ways, connected. The access we have to information simply boggles the mind compared to what it was a mere 15 years ago.

This progress, however, has come at a cost. Simply stated, our lives are not as private as they used to be. In some cases, it's the result of information or images that wind up in places we didn't expect (the most egregious example being "racey" photos). In other cases, our identities are being stolen by shady characters. In this latter case, others are literally pretending to be you. This is real and no laughing matter.

Identity theft is when an imposter uses your personal information without your permission. It's a crime and can cause untold problems for the victim. Generally speaking, it's caused by lost or stolen credit cards, careless disposal of investment/banking statements, providing personal information (Social Security Number and PINs) where you shouldn't, and various viral and malware attacks. The perpetrator may open credit cards and accounts in your name, forge your signature, and even obtain a driver's license in your name.

There is an ever-growing list of ways to avoid identity theft. It's impossible to mention them all, but some of the key ones are:

- Shredding your financial documents after their use
- Keeping PINs (for debit cards) and passwords in a safe, private place

MANAGING YOUR FINANCES

- Signing credit cards immediately and destroying outdated ones promptly
- Not including your Social Security Card in your wallet or purse
- Not disclosing your Social Security Number unless it is absolutely required
- Calling your financial institutions and credit card providers immediately if your wallet or purse is stolen
- Never taking phone solicitations that seek your Social Security Number and never emailing your Social Security Number or PINs to anyone.
- Only opening email attachments when you are **certain** as to their safety
- Treating your personal information as personal and private!
- Being extremely wary of phone solicitations. If offers sound too good to be true or the sales party is aggressive, steer clear! Personally, I just avoid solicitors altogether. Period.
- Report suspicious behavior immediately
- Use the best anti-virus and anti-malware software for your computers

Finally, there will be situations when you simply don't know if it's a safe bet. Here, you should consult with trusted people in the know before releasing any information that is private. Always err on the conservative.

TAKE FIVE: ›› How careful are you with your personal, financial, and computer information? Commit to keeping your private information private. May there always be only one you!

235

Apply

Give the "rainbow highlighter" study method a try using your own textbook(s) and preparing for a real exam. See how much more you recall after studying this way.

Words to Live By

Wise people treasure knowledge . . . —Proverbs 10:14

Journal

You can use the spaces below to record your thoughts, ideas, and reflections from your personal prayer times as you work through the section on "College Academics."

OUTCOMES OF THIS SECTION

After this section on "College Academics," you should be able to:

▌ Be committed to good planning, preparation, and performance in your academic pursuits

▌ Know how to plan a schedule and maintain a calendar

▌ Apply the rainbow highlighter study method to any test preparation

Chapter 6 — CAREER SELECTION AND ADVANCEMENT

*Choose your major/career after conducting a comprehensive assessment of yourself and potential career matches * Consider if it's a career, hobby, or volunteer opportunity * Build a winning competitive edge * Seek the wisdom of experienced pros * Demonstrate the qualities employers value * Learn to persuasively market yourself * Likeability during the interview is huge * Consider career advancement opportunities when evaluating offers * Learn the secret to a glowing performance evaluation! * Diversify your contributions to build your value and win promotions*

> *It is a good thing to receive wealth from God and the good health to enjoy it. To enjoy your work and accept your lot in life—this is indeed a gift from God. —Ecclesiastes 5:19*

Choosing your career is, without a doubt, one of the most important decisions you'll ever make in your life. This is no overstatement. It will determine your livelihood and how you'll use your God-given gifts, talents, and skills to realize your dreams. It will also influence how you spend much of your waking hours. This is a big deal so you'll want to get it right!

You have what it takes to thrive in a career that inspires you.

You'll need to be diligent, thorough, and objective as you evaluate career choices. Interestingly, there are countless careers that you'd excel at, but that doesn't mean they're the best overall fit for you. Too many people compromise when making this decision and get stuck in a job that bores them silly. That's why it's important that you surround yourself with people who believe *in* you (and believe *with* you). YOU HAVE WHAT IT TAKES to thrive in a career that inspires you. So, go for it!

Finally, selecting a great career match is only the beginning. You have to develop your qualifications, land a great job, and advance in it to your heart's desire. If you do this well, (and you can!), you will find great satisfaction and be well on your way to fulfilling God's plan for your life. Don't settle for anything less.

OBJECTIVES:

❚ Think about and start to plan for your eventual college major and/or career
❚ Understand and build your competitive edge and demonstrate the qualities that employers value
❚ Be able to market yourself to prospective employers
❚ Develop ways to build your value to an employer and learn the secrets of winning promotions

 **Prepare**

▌ Read Chapter Eight ("Career Selection and Advancement") in *What I Wish I Knew at 18*, starting on page 159.

▌ Use your highlighter pen to mark any sections that jump out at you— things you want to remember, take note of, or consider later.

▌ In the chart below, identify the pointers from the chapter that you con- sider to be:

      1. the most important in life
      2. ones you think you are already doing well and can model to others
      3. ones you either find the most challenging or in which you may
         need guidance to apply to your life

---

1. the most important in life

---

2. ones you think you are already doing well and can model to others

---

3. ones you either find the most challenging or in which you may need guidance to apply to your life

POINTER #1 —
CHOOSE YOUR MAJOR/CAREER AFTER CONDUCTING A COMPREHENSIVE ASSESSMENT OF YOURSELF AND POTENTIAL CAREER MATCHES

 ## Consider

There are a number of important factors to consider when identifying your future career and the path that will get you there. You may already have an idea of the type of work you'd like to pursue or the fields that interest you. Unfortunately, many develop these ideas without really knowing what that career field or job *actually* entails. They end up in a career mismatch or extending their college years in search of a better fit. Either way, it's regrettable.

Here are some *specific* things you need to evaluate as you consider career alternatives:

- Do I have a genuine interest in the subject area?
- Am I functionally gifted in that career area?
- What is the job outlook for that career (supply and demand)?
- Am I satisfied with the compensation that is typical for that career?
- What are my opportunities to advance in this career?
- Am I willing to do what it takes to become qualified for that job/profession?
- What are my personal and/or lifestyle preferences that may influence my satisfaction with that career, such as:

  - **working by myself versus working with others**
  - **stress tolerance**
  - **location preference**
  - **comfort level with income fluctuation (different careers have different patterns of income)**
  - **desire to work in larger versus smaller settings**
  - **workload demands and hours**

Because all of these variables contribute to overall career satisfaction, it is highly advisable to do your research before making a decision to select your college major, enlist in a branch of the military, sign up for a trade school, or make any other kind of decision about your career. Your research should include:

■ Talking to people who are already in that career about what their jobs and lives are like, their satisfaction with the career, the outlook for jobs, etc.

■ Investigating the current requirements and qualifications to serve in that career

■ Researching what schools offer the education you need, and what the costs and personal investment will be in terms of money and time

■ Doing a comprehensive self-assessment to determine if, in fact, you have the aptitude, skill set, and interest to work in that career

■ Prayerfully asking God for wisdom and guidance

In this chapter, we're going to help you do all of the above. You will start a binder in which you'll keep your research and any information or resources you acquire along the way. Are you ready? Let's get started!

 **Discuss**

In your small group, discuss the following questions (some may include activities to do together). Be honest and respect others' responses. There are no right or wrong answers and your group should be a safe place to talk and share freely.

1. Talk about the qualities of your ideal job.
2. What would you like to see yourself doing ten years from now?
3. Consider the subjects you like best in school. Which classes truly engage you? Which ones aren't so interesting? Are there areas of study you know you would definitely NOT want to go into? Which ones and why?
4. What majors or subject areas have you considered if you are thinking about college? Trades? Technical schools? Each person in your group should identify two or three potential matches for occupations or college majors and share them with the group.

**Apply**

Supplies needed: 1" or 1½" binder; four dividers; loose leaf paper; four clear plastic page protector sleeves for storing brochures, articles, business cards, or other resources you acquire.

In your career binder, make four sections using the dividers: Self Assessment, Research, Interviews, and Education. Place some looseleaf paper in each section, along with a clear plastic page protector sleeve. You will need all these for your career planning project. As you work through this section, continue to add any ideas or information you come across.

Consider

The job market has changed in recent decades, making the way we determine our career field and eventual profession more important than ever. That's why it's important you take this process seriously. Don't let anyone else do it for you, or talk you out of it. It's *your* life. No one knows you like you do. And whatever career you choose, you're the one who has to live with it.

And, it pays to consider that we are a "knowledge economy" with substantial differences in compensation depending on your years of schooling. Need proof? Check out the following table and you'll see the enormous lifetime differences in income based on years of education.[5] (We think you will want to finish high school!)

AVERAGE EARNINGS ACCORDING TO LEVEL OF EDUCATION		
	(Average) Annual Earnings	Lifetime Earnings (42 years)
HS dropout, no degree	$19,226	$ 807,492
HS diploma	$28,950	$1,215,900
Two-year college associate's degree	$36,395	$1,528,590
Four-year college bachelor's degree	$51,568	$2,165,856
Post-graduate degree (6+ years)	$67,073	$2,817,066

For your career planning project, you'll be completing a number of steps that will prepare you for the reality of the career you're considering. This will include taking an honest inventory of your current situation and outlook, as well as doing research and looking at options and strategies for the way forward. Each component of this process will be recorded in your career planning binder in the following sections:

SELF ASSESSMENT

Conduct a comprehensive self-assessment. Record your answers to the following prompts and questions in the "Self Assessment" section of your binder.

▍ *Interests and passions.* Think about which fields (e.g., medicine, business, education, performing arts) interest and excite you. What are they and why? Are you analytical? Persuasive? Creative? Organized? Relational? Mechanical? *Never* choose a major or career that may bore you!

▍ *Skills and aptitudes.* Just because you're interested in an area doesn't mean you have the required skills. You need to thoroughly understand your strengths and weaknesses and find an area that plays to your unique skill set and abilities. What are your greatest skills (things you can actually *do*)? How about aptitudes (these are areas in which you may not have actual skills, but that you know you would likely be good at)? Note that certain skills come naturally while others can be acquired with proper training. Regardless, it's critical to select a career in which you can excel.

▍ *Lifestyle and workplace preferences.* Identify your personal preferences regarding location, work hours, travel requirements, desired income, work style (individual versus team), and stress level. Your career has to fit who you are.

▍ *Willingness to obtain the necessary qualifications.* Some careers require only an undergraduate degree, while others (e.g., physicians) require extensive additional education and training. Even if you have the interest and skill, if you aren't willing to do what it takes to become qualified, it's not worth pursuing. How much time and effort are you willing to put toward your career?

Note: Your school counselor or career center may have a comprehensive self-assessment tool for your use or be able to give you access to one online. If so, substitute that exercise for this step—or better yet, do both to make sure you cover all the bases.

RESEARCH

Develop a list of potential careers that captures your interests, skills, and personal preferences. Learn about the qualifications for each career possibility and consider whether you have the skills and/or are willing to acquire them. Meet with admissions counselors and relevant faculty. Attend career fairs. Review the recommendations from any aptitude tests you've completed. Speak with others who know you best to hear their perspectives.

Investigate the demand outlook for the careers you're considering. This is an essential step because the global economy is constantly changing. New industries emerge (e.g., social networking) and mature industries decline (e.g., autos). Do your research to discover which careers are experiencing strong job growth. Don't invest in a dead end road.

INTERVIEWS

Talk to people in that field (or fields). As your list narrows, meet with actual practitioners in each career area to learn what the job is like, the qualifications, advancement potential, and what it takes to succeed. By speaking with people in that specific career, you'll receive invaluable, real-world perspectives.

Seek out work study or internship opportunities to get a flavor of what the career is actually like. This will provide a firsthand reality check and either confirm or reject your preliminary conclusions.

EDUCATION

Discover which schools offer programs in the field(s) you're considering. Check websites and course catalogs. Contact the school directly and talk to a counselor about your potential interest in the school and request an information packet.

Know and understand the requirements (and deadlines) for college entrance and financial aid. Have you written the SAT or ACT exam? If you will be seeking financial aid, have your parents completed the FAFSA (Free Application for Federal Student Aid)? Do you want to apply for scholarships or financial aid either from your school of choice or privately? These exams and applications have deadlines and you'll need to be aware of them. A good website to explore and register with (to help you with deadlines, information, research, and college planning) is www.collegeboard.org. Be sure, too, that you WRITE DOWN all application deadlines and deadlines for admission, scholarship, and financial aid applications. Record these in the Education section of your binder.

 **Discuss**

Do you already have a vague idea of the career you want? Here's a group exercise in which you can all take turns imagining what interviewing for your eventual dream job might be like.

1. Put yourself in the position of a hiring manager in the field you are considering. Imagine 30 candidates have applied for the job but you can ONLY PICK ONE.
2. Think about the qualities you will seek (experience, qualifications, and credentials) to fill that position.

3. Next, imagine yourself as YOU, applying for that job. What qualifications and experiences will you need in order to be the best candidate for the job? Would YOU hire YOU? There's only one right answer to that question!

4. What can you start doing NOW to position yourself to be their top choice (e.g., education, critical skills, internships, volunteering, personal qualities, professional connections, experiences)?

Discuss these scenarios and your thoughts and ideas with the rest of your group. Help each other come up with suggestions for item #4 above and record these in the Journal at the end of this section.

 **Apply**

Like every journey in life, career choice and advancement have a beginning, a middle, and an end. Many people think the beginning starts with the choices you make *after* high school—not true! You can begin now to identify pathways and objectives that will take you where you want to go, or at least get you started in the right direction.

You can begin now to identify pathways and objectives that will take you where you want to go, or at least get you started in the right direction.

A great research tool is the Bureau of Labor Statistic's *Occupational Outlook Handbook*, which you can find at www.bls.gov/oco. On this site you will find the descriptions for hundreds of occupations, in addition to the education and training you'll need to qualify for them. Also listed are average earnings and future projections for growth in each profession. Need help starting to identify which jobs and careers might be a good fit for you? Check out this website: www.bls.gov/k12/index.htm. It's called, "What Do You Like?" and can help you narrow down your options based on your own interests.

Here's another idea: after the discussion with your small group about your ideal job, look up some of your selections in the *Occupational Outlook Handbook*. Record some of your findings in the Research section of your career binder.

Look up some of your selections in the *Occupational Outlook Handbook*. Record some of your findings in the Research section of your career binder.

▮ What surprises you?
▮ What interests you?
▮ Has anything caused you to reconsider your previous choices?

POINTER #2 —
BUILD A WINNING COMPETITIVE EDGE AND DEMONSTRATE THE QUALITIES THAT EMPLOYERS VALUE

 Consider

Our world is much more competitive than ever before. Gone is the day when our economy was built on manufacturing and manual labor jobs that didn't require a post-high school education. In those days, workers were paid by the hour and there was little differentiation in wages. However, our economy has become service-oriented and knowledge-based, which has changed everything. Now, you have to demonstrate something special (i.e., skills, educational credentials, experiences, and achievements) in order to land the job and advance in your career. Together, these make up your competitive edge.

You need to be able to demonstrate something special (i.e., skills, experiences, and achievements) in order to land the job and advance in your career.

You'll gain two significant benefits from building your competitive edge. First, you'll expand your skill set and become more marketable, promotable, and valuable. Second, you'll show employers that you're passionate about your work and are driven to perform. Give an employer a great skill set and a winning attitude, and you'll be a success story in the making!

What do we mean by a "competitive edge?" It means:

- Considering what would stand out about you to future employers
- Going the extra mile to become better qualified through experiences and continuing education
- If lacking a skill or a professional qualification, attacking it with full force
- Demonstrating an attitude of continuous improvement and a commitment to excellence
- Showing significant accomplishments and impact and exceeding the qualifications for the position

As you progress along your career path, it's important to demonstrate the character qualities that are highly valued by employers.

Additionally, as you progress along your career path, it's important to demonstrate the character qualities that are highly valued by employers. Review the qualities of true workplace VIPs in *What I Wish I Knew at 18* (page 173) and take them to heart. By doing so, you'll increase your chances of getting hired and advance more rapidly, and sidestep those nasty layoffs during economic downturns!

 # Discuss

Imagine yourself as an owner of a business that employs many people. Brainstorm and see how many positive attributes of valuable employees you can come up with as a group and add them to the list on page 173 of *What I Wish I Knew at 18.* As a boss, which ones would be the most important to you? Next, do the opposite. What do you think are the most UNDESIRABLE qualities in an employee? Come up with a top ten and a worst ten list. Compare your answers with the rest of the class.

 # Apply

Looking back at the list of qualities that employers value, rate yourself on a scale of one to five for each quality, five being "star performer" and one being "you've got a ways to go." Ask someone who knows you well (but is not a peer) to do the same. Do others see you the same way you see yourself? Circle the top three qualities you think you need to work on and begin a plan to make a fresh start in those areas.

 # Words to Live By

Work willingly at whatever you do, as though you were working for the Lord rather than for people. Remember that the Lord will give you an inheritance as your reward, and that the Master you are serving is Christ. —Colossians 3:23–24

POINTER #3 —
LEARN TO PERSUASIVELY MARKET YOURSELF/LIKEABILITY DURING THE INTERVIEW IS HUGE

 Consider

Wouldn't it be nice if we could just go through life minding our own business and have others automatically recognize our greatness by offering us jobs, scholarships, promotions (complete with big bucks!), and the like? Unfortunately, it usually doesn't work out that way.

In order to land that perfect job or win that prized promotion over others, you must persuade people that *you* are the answer to what they're looking for. As pointed out earlier, much of life is a competition—and you need to persuasively market yourself in order to successfully compete. You need to become an effective salesperson of . . . YOU!

You need to become an effective salesperson of . . . YOU!

Here are some pointers to help you get started in learning to persuasively market yourself in the job market. Whether it's a summer job or the first stop in your career journey, these tips will serve you well.

▌ Consider how your assets address the prospective employer's needs. *Think of yourself as the solution to their problem.*

▌ Build a compelling resume that highlights your strongest accomplishments and competitive advantages.

▌ Network with as many people as you can to receive endorsements and inside connections.

▌ During interviews, be personable, confident but not arrogant, look your interviewer in the eye, repeat their name, shake their hand firmly, listen intently, come prepared with questions, show an interest in the company and the job, ask for a business card, promptly send a thank you note, exhibit confident body language, be yourself, and smile.

▌ Remember that the first 30 seconds of a job interview will make or break your chances of landing the job. They may not get you the offer, but they will certainly kill your chances if you don't make a strong first impression. Get off to the right start by being friendly, positive, enthusiastic, humble, relaxed, and natural. Be professional in your appearance and in your grammar.

Discuss

Conduct mock job interviews. Everyone in the group should get a chance to play the role of either the interviewer or interviewee (preferably both, if time allows). Choose from the questions on page 174 of *What I Wish I Knew at 18* (also listed below). Each candidate should be required to answer three to five questions from the list, depending on time. Before you begin, allow a few minutes for everyone to get a head start. Interviewees should be prepared to honestly answer:

▌ What value can you bring to the table?
▌ What are your strengths and weaknesses?
▌ Why should we hire you? Why are you interested in the job?
▌ What do you consider to be your greatest accomplishments and personal attributes?
▌ What motivates you?
▌ What are you passionate about?
▌ What's the most difficult challenge you ever faced, and how did you deal with it?
▌ What three adjectives best describe you as a person?

Offer constructive feedback, considering the quality of their answers as well as how they came across to you as the hiring manager. What was it like to be interviewed? Which questions were easier or harder to answer? With more practice and good "talking points," you'll get better and better at interviews.

Apply

▌ Make a list of all of your strengths, qualifications, experiences, and accomplishments.
▌ Consider why they would be valuable to an employer.
▌ Identify some personal stories that convey your positive attitude, unique achievements, and commitment to excellence.
▌ Develop a resume to include with your job applications when you apply for jobs. There are some excellent online sites that can help you, and Microsoft Word® has templates to make it even easier.
▌ Note that resumes are not restricted to the job market. Are you an athlete hoping to market yourself to the coaching staff of a desired university? You can make a sports resume. Simply adapt the above criteria with a view to communicating (and marketing) your athletic abilities and contributions. The same goes for music, drama, and other fields.

POINTER #4 —
DIVERSIFY YOUR CONTRIBUTIONS TO BUILD YOUR VALUE AND WIN PROMOTIONS

 Consider

You've no doubt heard the saying, "Beauty is in the eyes of the beholder." Well, when it comes to your career, your *value* is in the eyes of your *employer*. How highly prized you are to your employer should be a matter of ongoing importance. It affects your pay, promotion potential, professional reputation, and job security, so it's a big deal!

Among the sources of your value are your:

- Proficiency and achievement on the job
- Contribution to the financial well-being of the organization
- Ability to develop others
- Ability to work successfully in teams and in projects
- Ability to solve problems and lead initiatives
- Willingness to go above and beyond the job description

In a nutshell, it's not simply how well you're doing your own job, but also how you're contributing to the broader enterprise. As you progress in your career, always ask what you can do to become more valuable to your employer. The answers will help separate you from the crowd.

It's not simply how well you're doing your own job, but also how you're contributing to the broader enterprise.

 Discuss

Similar to the exercise you did earlier in this chapter, imagine another job interview—only this time you are not applying for the original *job*, you're now being interviewed for a *promotion*.

1. Put yourself in the position of being a supervising manager in the company you've been working at since you graduated and found a job in your chosen field. Imagine three existing employees are being considered for a promotion, along with several outside applicants. You can ONLY PICK ONE.

2. Think about what qualities, achievements, and accomplishments you are going to look for (see the list in Pointer #4 above) to fill that position.

3. Next, imagine yourself as YOU, being considered for that promotion, along with two of your co-workers and several outside applicants. What do you want to have accomplished, what kind of reputation do you want to have built, and what do you want to be recognized for that will make YOU the most qualified for the promotion?

4. What kinds of things should you have been doing in your job to get yourself to the place where YOU are the one who gets that promotion (e.g., continuing education, seeking out a mentor, looking for opportunities to participate in special projects, going above and beyond your job description, networking)?

Discuss these scenarios and your thoughts and ideas with the rest of your group. Help each other come up with suggestions for item #4 above and record these in the Journal at the end of this section along with your responses from the earlier exercise.

 **Apply**

Look at the lists you compiled in the Journal section of this chapter (or in your career binder), consisting of things that you can do (or can eventually do) to make yourself more marketable, valuable, and promotable. Using a highlighter pen, highlight three that you can start working on RIGHT NOW.

How are you going to accomplish these? Come up with at least one idea for each. Then compare your list to others in your group. Do you all have suggestions for one another?

Journal

You can use the spaces below to record your thoughts, ideas, and reflections from your personal prayer times as you work through the chapter on "Career Selection and Advancement."

OUTCOMES OF THIS SECTION

▮ Start on your research and plan for pursuing your eventual college major and/or future career by compiling a career binder

▮ Know how to build a competitive edge and demonstrate the qualities that employers value

▮ Be able to market yourself to employers

▮ Once you've landed a job, know ways to build your value to an employer and win promotions

Continue to reflect on the other pointers you read in this chapter of the book, *What I Wish I Knew at 18,* which may not be included in this student manual. The "Take Five" sections are especially helpful to gauge how that particular pointer might be of help or encouragement to you. Don't skip them . . . they may just turn out to be the best part!

Chapter 7 — LOVE AND MARRIAGE

*Take a "3-D" approach to dating * Recognize the difference between love and lust * Love takes time . . . and timing! * Choose your spouse as a forever decision * Fully explore your compatibility before committing * Don't expect your spouse to change his/her ways * Maintain your friendships after marriage * Marriage is a partnership that requires continual investment * Learn key words for a successful marriage * Have children when you're married and ready * Commit to making these life choices to avoid poverty*

> *Marriage is to be held in honor among all . . .*
> *—Hebrews 13:4*

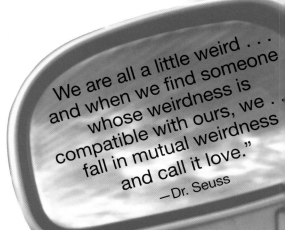

We are all a little weird . . . and when we find someone whose weirdness is compatible with ours, we . . . fall in mutual weirdness and call it love."
—Dr. Seuss

One of the most significant aspects of your life involves love relationships and, very likely, marriage. Marriage is part of God's design for life on earth. "It is not good for man to be alone," God said at the very beginning (Genesis 2:18). Isn't it cool that one of the very first things God knew man needed was—a mate? Love, marriage, sex . . . it was all God's idea from the very beginning, and the Bible talks about it a lot (and how to handle it). But like anything else created by design, you need to operate that part of your life according to its original plan and purpose—or things can go terribly wrong.

During your teen years, you start to notice that there are different kinds of love. There is the kind of love you have for (and receive from) your parents and, hopefully, your siblings. (If you're not feeling the love from your siblings right now, don't worry; that will likely change as you grow into adulthood.) There is the kind of "love" you feel for your closest friends (even if you don't call it that). But there is another kind of loving emotion—romantic love if you want to call it that—that starts to come to the forefront during this season of your life. It's an intense, nothing-like-it experience, and whether or not it actually turns into Real Love only time will tell. But when it does, it can be the foundation for the most important human relationship you may ever have—marriage.

It's never too soon to start thinking about and preparing for marriage (after all, many meet their eventual spouse within a few years after high school).

Though marriage probably seems pretty far off right now, it's never too soon to start thinking about and preparing for this important decision (after all, many meet their eventual spouse within a few years after high school!). Interestingly, researchers have found that the building blocks of healthy adult marriages are formed during the teenage years. This means you can start now to discover what love really means, learn how to gauge your compatibility with someone who is a potential boyfriend/girlfriend and eventual mate, and start to understand the investment required for a successful, lifelong marriage partnership. That's what this chapter is all about.

OBJECTIVES:

▮ Understand that God's plan for marriage is part of His original design for human society and needs to be planned for and entered into seriously

▮ Learn and apply a successful model to your dating relationships: be discerning, discriminating, and deliberate

▮ Understand that successful love relationships require time— and proper timing

▮ Learn the difference between love and lust

▮ Decide now to make your choice of mate a *forever* decision, and learn how to gauge your compatibility *before* committing to someone

▮ Learn some key principles for maintaining a successful marriage

 Prepare

▮ **Read Chapter 9 ("Love and Marriage") in *What I Wish I Knew at 18,* starting on page 183.**

▮ **Use your highlighter pen to highlight anything in the chapter that jumps out at you—things you want to remember, take note of, come back to, or discuss later.**

▮ **In the chart below, identify the pointers that meet the following criteria:**

1. the ones you think are the most important
2. the ones you think you are already mindful of
3. the ones you find most challenging or are new ideas for you

1. the ones you think are the most important

2. the ones you think you are already mindful of

3. the ones you find most challenging or are new ideas for you

_____

_____

_____

_____

POINTER #1 —
TAKE A "3-D" APPROACH TO DATING

 Consider

When and how you start to date is a decision that varies from person to person and from family to family. Regardless of when and how you approach it, you need to know that responsible dating comes with its share of challenges. That's because:

1. By its nature, dating can be a "trial and error" process with many dead ends or worse.
2. There are two parties involved, each with his or her own unique needs, goals, feelings, and interests.
3. It's easy to lose objectivity when emotions take over.
4. Some people try so hard to please the other person that they'll compromise their values to stay together. Sadly, many define their self worth based on whether they're "together" with someone and struggle with loneliness, insecurity, and doubt when unattached.

With those caveats in mind, how can you be a responsible, sensible dater who gets the most out of relationship-building? Here's an idea. Take a "3-D" approach to dating by being:

Discriminating
Discerning
Deliberate

Be Discriminating

Being a discriminating dater means being highly selective (not dating just for dating's sake), and includes knowing the qualities you admire and that attract you to another person. If you don't see a fit, move on.

Be Discerning

Be wise when you date. Too many people approach dating impulsively and emotionally and simply don't think clearly. It also means avoiding situations that risk challenging your values. Try to model the practices of a discerning dater (listed in *What I Wish I Knew at 18,* pages 192–193).

Be Deliberate

If the relationship is truly meant to be, it needn't be rushed. If the other person wants things to move much faster than you, consider it a red flag, as difficult as this may be. It's probably a sign that it's either a poor match or simply not the right time. Almost everyone goes through situations like this. It hurts in the short run to break up, but it's better in the long run not to delay the inevitable.

 Discuss

In your small group, discuss the following questions (some may include activities to do together). Be honest and respect others' responses. There are no right or wrong answers and your group should be a safe place to talk and share freely.

This time, separate into your small groups by gender (boys with boys, girls with girls). Talk about the following questions in your group. If time allows, share your group's answers with the larger group when you're finished to see the differing perspectives.

▐ What is important to you in a relationship?
▐ What qualities do you find attractive (*not* talking about physical attributes here)?
▐ What are some essential qualities in someone you would consider dating?
▐ Are there some qualities that are not essential but desirable? What are they?
▐ What are your deal-breakers—qualities that are definitely **not** for you?
▐ What are some good dating activities/ideas for people who want to be "3-D" daters?
▐ What are the pros and cons of deciding not to date at all during certain seasons of your life?

 Words to Live By

Above all else, guard your heart, for it is the wellspring of life. (Proverbs 4:23, NIV)

 **Apply**

Look back over the values list that you compiled in Chapter Two of this study guide. Which of them do you consider non-negotiable "must haves" for anyone you would date (and potentially marry)? Which are "nice but not necessary?" Which are "don't matter at all?" In the chart below, fill in the appropriate columns with those qualities.

Need To Have	Nice To Have	Don't Want

POINTER #2 —
LOVE TAKES TIME—AND TIMING!

 Consider

While infatuation can occur in a moment, it takes a *long* time to *really* get to know someone and truly gauge if he or she is a candidate for something deeper. When you contemplate the pointer, "Fully explore your compatibility before committing," you'll see that it takes significant time to gauge whether you have a perfect match. That means lots of conversations, experiences, and observation. You need to know that the Hollywood "three days and we're engaged" routine doesn't really work in the long term. It takes *time* for real love to solidify and grow. As tough as it is, you need to be patient. If your relationship is truly meant to be, it will happen.

You also need to consider timing. During the teen and young adult years, people are going through the greatest time of self-discovery in their lives. At the end of that time period, you don't even have the same person you started off with because people change so much during this time. The timing of a committed love relationship may not be right during this often turbulent season of life.

The timing issue is always more fundamental if we're in a season of change, or have a lot going on in our life, are on the rebound from a previous relationship, or are not able to place the necessary priority a serious relationship deserves. It may not mean this relationship is a "not ever" one; it may just be a "not now" one.

You also need to know that the timing may not be right at certain seasons of your life for you to date at all—and that's okay. Too often young adults get trapped into the notion that they always need to have a love interest. No so! Don't let your self-worth and significance be tied to whether or not you have a date on Friday night. And don't hesitate to step off the dating treadmill if you need to or want to . . . you don't always have to be actively dating or have a steady boyfriend or girlfriend.

Don't hesitate to step off the dating treadmill if you need to or want to . . . you don't always have to be actively dating or have a steady boyfriend or girlfriend.

 # Words to Live By

Better a patient person than a warrior, one with self-control than one who takes a city.
—*Proverbs 16:32*

Here's a great exercise that can help you pace yourself in relationships, and be discerning about what levels of trust and propriety are appropriate at which levels.

The 4 Stages of Relationships

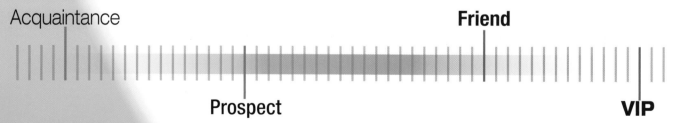

Acquaintance   Friend   Prospect   VIP

Generally speaking, most relationships go through four stages and, ideally, each stage should build on the other. **What takes a relationship to new stages or levels are: trust, compatibility, and a shared interest in making it so.** Every person who becomes more than an acquaintance will start in the first stage. Many stay there forever. Some may grow into the next stage and the next. Only a very few will make it to the fourth stage—and that's the way it should be.

Unfortunately, many people—particularly young and inexperienced people—can rush the stages, moving from one to the next prematurely in the rush to intimacy or by succumbing to pressure. Or, they can exhibit behaviors in one stage that are inappropriate for that level of relationship, which should be reserved for a deeper or intimate one. Here are the stages:

Stage One—Acquaintance (someone you don't know well)

Characteristics of this stage: being very careful how you're behaving around (or being perceived by) the other person, not wanting to offend or alienate them in any way, sometimes even being overly anxious to please or have the other person find you attractive/acceptable, trust level is very guarded, you avoid conflict at all costs.

Stage Two—Prospect (a potential friend)

Characteristics of this stage: finding common interests, exchanging contact information, starting to communicate spontaneously, conversations are generally fairly superficial and don't go to deep personal issues; you may exchange socially-accepted physical gestures of greeting (such as a handshake) but they are very casual and tempered; you still avoid conflict; trust level is raised but still fairly cautionary (Each person is wondering, "Can I trust you? Are you a long-term person in my life or not?").

Stage Three—Friend

Characteristics of this stage: developing higher levels of trust, seeing each other's differences and shortcomings and sticking with the relationship anyway, expressing and receiving honest opinions and negotiating conflict successfully, demonstrating genuine affection, sharing thoughts and feelings safely, more self-disclosure and vulnerability, developing shared activities and interests that you do together regularly and possibly exclusively with that person only, and finding common interests and values.

Stage Four—VIP

Imagine your relationships in a pyramid, with this level being the very small piece at the top. Relatively few people in your lifetime will make it to this level. You may not realize this yet, but you don't have to have fifty million best friends! No one does! It's not about quantity; it's quality that counts at this level. When it comes to the top of the pyramid, that's reserved for very special people in your life.

You will have several kinds of relationships in this upper level. Familial VIPs are inherited; the closeness of your upbringing gives you a connection that is unique. They are not just invested in you,

but you are invested in them as a part of your genetic mini-community, which is your family. That takes it to a different level that wouldn't be the same for your friends or romantic relationships.

For the average person, there are more people at the VIP level that are the same gender as you; people with whom you have total trust, loyalty, and bonding. For romantic relationships, this level is reserved for the super serious, either in or headed toward marriage.

A MAJOR WORD OF CAUTION!

Don't rush to this stage (like they do in the movies). When you do, you take a big risk of making an emotional investment without really knowing the person—a mistake that may have a high emotional cost later when you break up. It's better to go slowly through the stages and reserve this level for people who really prove their friendship, commitment, and compatibility over time.

 **Discuss**

For discussion in your small group:

1. Do you agree that all your relationships fall somewhere on this spectrum?
2. What do you think happens when people rush or mix up the stages?
3. How would you respond if someone began behaving toward you as if you and he/she were in stage three (or even four), when in your own mind you only feel comfortable with him or her as a stage two?
4. Having good boundaries means you know what is appropriate for each relational stage and you will not act (or put up with others acting) out of line with what is acceptable for that level of relationship. What happens when people don't have good boundaries?
5. After completing this Pointer, do you understand why true love takes *time*? Explain.
6. As a group, take the following list of behaviors and assign them to the most appropriate relational stage. You may have differences of opinions as to which belong where. Each person should be prepared to defend his or her ideas.

   ▌ Giving out your phone number
   ▌ Talking on the phone (long conversations)
   ▌ Sharing your deepest feelings, secrets, and experiences
   ▌ Praying with and for one another

- Being "friends" on Facebook®
- Hanging out with the other person in groups
- Communicating disappointment or criticism
- Hanging out with the other person one-on-one
- Texting
- PDAs (public displays of affection)
- Spending time with each other's families
- Being exclusive with that person (not dating any other people)
- Being blunt/very direct with your opinions
- Expressing strong emotions like anger, fear, or grief
- If a potentially romantic relationship, one-on-one "dates"
- Going on a weekend camping trip

 **Apply**

Are you dating someone right now? Here's a quick checklist recapping the principles in this section. How many of them can you answer so far? Which ones do you need to further explore?

- Can they be trusted?
- How do they behave under stress?
- Are they willing to share their feelings or do they bury them inside?
- Do they share similar goals, views, interests, and values?
- Do they have an authentic and demonstrable faith in Jesus Christ?
- Do they have any dependencies?
- What are their career interests and ambitions?
- Are they interested in marriage and having a family someday?
- Do they respect your values and boundaries?
- How much of your attraction is toward the inside versus the outside and the physical versus the non-physical?

POINTER #3 —
RECOGNIZE THE DIFFERENCE BETWEEN LOVE AND LUST

 Consider

How do you know you when you're in love? That, frankly, is an age-old question! Love is such a powerful human emotion that psychologists, counselors, faith leaders, and even doctors and scientists are constantly studying it. Some key words and phrases that describe "love" include the following:

▌ Enduring emotional regard for another
▌ Steadfast loyalty
▌ Strong affection arising out of kinship or personal ties
▌ Admiration, benevolence, or common interests
▌ Unselfish loyalty and genuine concern for the good of another
▌ Putting another's interests ahead of your own

Do you notice how other-focused, deep, and non-physical "love" is?

Many times people will say they're in love when, really, they are in "lust." Some key words and phrases that would describe lust might include:

▌ Passionate or overwhelming desire
▌ Craving another
▌ Intense or unbridled sexual desire or appetite

Do you notice how self-centered, impatient, and physical "lust" is?

When you enter the whole dating scene, knowing what true love *really* is can be confusing—and overwhelming. So, it helps to have an idea of what you're looking for. You also need to identify and commit to maintaining your standards—before you get into situations that might compromise them. Your standards for sexual purity should come from Scripture, not from peer pressure (i.e., "everyone else is doing it") or from your own emotions (which are often not an accurate gauge of reality or wisdom, especially in the heat of the moment). The Bible makes it clear that sexual relationships outside of marriage are against God's design (see Matthew 19:4–6; 1 Corinthians 6:16–20; 7:2; Ephesians 5:31).

Additionally, Jesus continually emphasized that sin *starts* in the heart. If the heart is pure, then actions will also be pure. He said that anger toward your brother is like murder; adultery is as simple as having lust in the heart.

So what does the real thing—real love—*look* like? Research indicates that romantic love—the kind that may eventually lead to the lifelong partnership of marriage—can be understood in three components: attraction, closeness, and commitment.

Attraction is the chemistry part of love. It's all about the physical—even sexual—interest that two people have in each other. Sometimes we think when we feel *attraction* that this is *love*. But at

this point it can more accurately be called *infatuation* or even, if it's especially intense, *lust*. Love involves much more than a physical attraction—although that's certainly part of it.

Closeness is the emotional bond that develops when we share thoughts and feelings with that special someone that we may not share with anyone else. It involves supporting, caring for, honoring, understanding, praying for, and accepting the other person for who he or she is (and vice versa). It also involves learning to trust one another.

Commitment is when we choose to stay with the other person through the ups and downs of the relationship and, possibly, through the ups and downs of life. We up the ante, so to speak, with our commitment level.

You can experience these three components of love in different combinations in different kinds of relationships. You might have:

1. Closeness without attraction—like you might share with a best friend
2. Attraction without closeness—a "crush" or infatuation; if very intense can be characterized as "lust"
3. Attraction combined with closeness—romantic love
4. Attraction combined with closeness and commitment—potential for marriage

Especially for people who may be experiencing attraction, infatuation, and love for the first time, it can be hard to tell the difference between the three. It doesn't help that the media and culture repeatedly send misleading and distorted messages about what love really is.

Don't let anyone fool you: Love is NOT sex. Love isn't just a bundle of intense feelings, emotions, and attraction. It's all of the deeper elements described in the first description mentioned above. Learn to know the difference. Your most important love relationship depends on it!

 **Discuss**

Get into small groups of the same gender again. In your group, discuss the following questions (some may include activities to do together). Be honest and respect others' responses. There are no right or wrong answers and your group should be a safe place to talk and share freely.

Surveys indicate that older teens and young adults say the number one reason to marry is for love. Talk about definitions of love—both the ones cited in this chapter and others you may have heard elsewhere. Discuss good and bad examples of love from life, media (including music, TV, and movies), and society. Also discuss the following questions:

▮ How can you know the difference between attraction, lust, and love?
▮ How do you think God's definition of love (see 1 Corinthians 13:4–7) might differ from the world's definition of love?

▌ How do you know whether or not to believe someone who says he or she "loves" you?

▌ How is real love formed, sustained, and nurtured over time?

▌ Is attraction or lust enough to make a relationship successful? Is love?

▌ What else does it take to form a healthy relationship? Why?

 **Apply**

It helps to have someone to talk with about what you're experiencing and feeling when you think you're falling in love—someone older, wiser, and more experienced who has your best interests in mind, not just your peers. Find a trusted someone like a mature, "been-there-done-that" kind of person who can be a sounding board for you and give you objective advice.

 Above and Beyond

In your personal prayer time, talk to God about your commitment to purity and to maintaining His standards for your relationships with the opposite sex. Make some decisions now about steps you will take to maintain that commitment. Ask Him to help you.

If you have already made some mistakes and violated your own standards, don't be discouraged. There is no such thing as one sin that is worse than another. It doesn't make Him love you any less. However, generally speaking, some sins do have more serious (practical) consequences than others. Sexual sin can lead to other serious and devastating things like disease, illegitimate pregnancies, and abortion. It may involve adultery, divorce, and the destruction of marriages and families. Sex, which is a marvelous design of God for pleasure and unity in marriage, becomes a ticking time bomb when exercised outside of its God-given parameters.

If you've made some mistakes, take Him at His word that He is compassionate, slow to anger, and quick to forgive (see Psalm 103:8–14). Ask for His forgiveness, which He is always happy to give (1 John 1:9) and start over with a clean slate and new commitment.

POINTER #4 —
CHOOSE YOUR SPOUSE AS A FOREVER DECISION/FULLY EXPLORE YOUR COMPATIBILITY BEFORE COMMITTING

 Consider

It's no secret that today's divorce rate is borderline astronomical, notwithstanding the expressions of love and commitment that each party spoke on their wedding day. Unfortunately, it seems, marriage has become part of our disposable society.

Marriage is one of the few decisions you'll make in your life that's meant to be *permanent*. That's why Jesus said, "But 'God made them male and female' from the beginning of creation. 'This explains why a man leaves his father and mother and is joined to his wife, and the two are united into one.' Since they are no longer two but one, *let no one split apart what God has joined together*" (Mark 10:6–9, emphasis added). That's a high bar and means we have to take marriage a lot more seriously than almost any other decision.

"**Love** one another and you will be **happy**. It's as **simple** and as **difficul[t]** as that."
—Michael Leunig

Marriage should be approached with the mindset that it will be forever. That means choosing your spouse with a *great* degree of care and working through the difficulties you'll face from time to time. If you do this, your odds of achieving a wonderful, lifelong relationship will measurably increase. And if, by chance, your own parents are no longer married to one another, that doesn't mean you can't have a forever marriage someday.

Part of the key to a lifelong marriage is proper *preparation*, part of it is *commitment*, and a great deal of it is *compatibility*. When it comes to important decisions like our colleges, majors, careers, house—and yes, our marriages—it pays to identify your key criteria. That way, when that special someone comes along, you can put him or her to the test and see if it survives.

Some people may say, "Love is blind." But don't let it be that way for you. Keep your eyes open. Be discerning and objective and consider the following:

Communication: The way a person communicates with you (or anyone else, really) will give you a clue of how your relationship will look as it progresses. Can he or she express opinions and feelings freely, clearly, and respectfully? The better the two of you are at communicating issues, the more successful your relationship will be.

Conflict resolution: The way a person handles and resolves conflicts is crucial and should influence whether you stay in a relationship or not. Are there anger management issues? Don't ever make excuses for someone hurting you either physically or verbally. It is an unacceptable way to resolve conflict and a warning sign that this is not the person for you.

Social skills: How does your prospective partner relate to other people? Are you comfortable with his or her level of social ability and comfort? Do you like the way he or she acts when around friends, and is it significantly different than how he/she acts around you? If so, that might be a warning sign that you are not seeing the real person.

Reaction to stress: When things get tough, how does the other person respond? How each of you copes with stress and adjusts to various circumstances will help in predicting whether you'll be able to have a satisfactory relationship with your prospective partner.

Character: How would you rate this person's integrity? Things like honesty, respect, work ethic, and dependability will make a huge difference in what kind of life partner he or she turns out to be. How does he/she relate to his/her parents? To teachers and other authority figures? Does he/she respect rules? Does he/she respect *your* boundaries? Watch out for the "little" things—they matter!

Values: Do you and this person share basic life values? If not, you are in for some ongoing tension in your relationship. Things like regard for and commitment to spiritual life, education, marriage and family, and so on are basic foundations of a successful, committed relationship. It takes time— and often the right questions, conversations, and situations—for these to emerge.

Does he or she have an authentic and demonstrable faith in Jesus Christ? If you are not both on the same page when it comes to your faith, it will eventually cause problems. The Bible cautions us on what it can be like to try and pull a load together with someone who is going in a totally different spiritual direction than we are. Basically, one will be inclined to go one way and the other another way, with the result being . . . problems! We would expect in such a situation to see disunity, frustration, and lack of progress—to say the least. That's why it's important to keep biblical principles in mind when you are considering or planning for marriage.

You also need to know that the need to evaluate your compatibility before you commit to marriage *doesn't* mean living together beforehand. Many people believe that if they live together before marriage (i.e., "testing the waters"), they can better determine their compatibility. Unfortunately, the opposite is more often true. Living together without the commitment of marriage tends to create a "back door escape" mentality that is difficult to break out of even after the couple actually marries.

A godly, lifelong marriage requires compatibility, shared faith, common purpose, and authentic commitment. With these ingredients in place, the chances of your marriage being a forever one are much more likely.

Discuss

Discuss in your small group:

- What do you think about marriage?
- Do you think you'll want to get married someday?
- Do you agree that marriage is intended to be "forever?" Why or why not?
- How important do you think it is that a Christian marry another Christian? Why?
- Why is it that the odds of a forever marriage are worse for a couple that lives together first? Isn't that counterintuitive? If this isn't in the best interests of a permanent marriage, why do you think it has become more culturally accepted?

Apply

What kind of marriage do *you* want? Describe the qualities of an ideal marriage relationship. Jot down a list in the "Journal" section of some of the qualities you will look for in a mate someday. Pray about these things and ask God to show you the person He has for you. Then hang on to your list—it will be fun to refer back to in a few years!

POINTER #5 — KEYWORDS FOR A SUCCESSFUL MARRIAGE

 Consider

With all the scary statistics out there, it may cause you to think that having a forever marriage is impossible. Not so! A successful marriage *is* attainable and you can plan for one now. Although marriage might be quite a way off, having an accurate vision for a successful marriage will help you prepare for that life decision. Here are some key words that represent qualities present in long-term relationships that have stayed the course. Run them through your own "values self-check." How many of them are already important to you? Which ones do you think would be the most challenging? Which might be the most common reasons for marriage failure?

- Commitment
- Respect
- Teamwork
- Shared faith
- Listening
- Forgiveness
- Communication
- Encouragement
- Investment
- Perseverance
- Fun

 Discuss

In your small group, talk about marriages you've seen that have been long-term ones—perhaps your parents or grandparents, maybe another relative or a family friend/neighbor. Swap stories and analyze the following together:

- What strikes you as most significant about this couple's relationship with one another?
- What do you admire about them?
- Look at the list of key words for a successful marriage in the list above. Which of these do you see in the marriages you've discussed?

Talk about movies you've seen that depict ultimately successful relationships. Were there common themes that helped the relationships endure? What do YOU think are the most important elements that will lead to a successful marriage for you?

 **Apply**

Actually *talk* to some couples who have been married for a long time. Conduct a mini-interview or two. Find out what key words they, personally, would identify as being significant in the success of their relationship. Would they identify any in their own marriage that are not on the list in Chapter Nine of *What I Wish I Knew at 18*?

 **Journal**

You can use the spaces below to record your thoughts, ideas, and reflections from your personal prayer times as you work through the section on "Love and Marriage."

OUTCOMES OF THIS SECTION

After this section on "Love and Marriage," you should be able to:

▌ Apply the "3-D" dating principles to your own dating relationships

▌ Recognize that successful love relationships require time—and proper timing

▌ Understand the difference between love and lust

▌ Determine how to gauge your compatibility before committing to someone, recognizing marriage is intended to be permanent

▌ Learn some key components of a successful marriage

Continue to reflect on the other pointers you read in this chapter of the book, *What I Wish I Knew at 18,* which may not be included in this student manual. The "Take Five" sections are especially helpful to gauge how that particular pointer might be of help or encouragement to you. Don't skip them . . . they may just turn out to be the best part!

Chapter 8 — **MANAGING YOUR FINANCES**

*Commit to your financial literacy ＊ **Strive to become a wise steward, disciplined saver, prudent consumer, cautious debtor, and cheerful giver** ＊ *Beware . . . even those with substantial assets can go bankrupt!* ＊ **Live within your means and generate positive cash flow** ＊ **Create regular cash flow statements and analyze your spending** ＊ **Use credit sparingly and wisely** ＊ **Develop a financial plan that reflects your short- and long-term goals** ＊ *Understand your ability to handle risk and invest accordingly* ＊ **Invest early, regularly, and as much as you can in a diversified, long-term strategy** ＊ *Build an emergency fund for unforeseen circumstances* ＊ **Grow your wealth patiently** ＊ *Build and maintain a good credit rating*

> *Teach those who are rich in this world not to be proud and not to trust in their money, which is so unreliable. Their trust should be in God, who richly gives us all we need for our enjoyment. Tell them to use their money to do good. They should be rich in good works and generous to those in need, always being ready to share with others. By doing this they will be storing up their treasure as a good foundation for the future so that they may experience true life. —1 Timothy 6:17–19*

Money, money, money. Few things in life generate as much interest yet demand more responsibility. When managed well, it provides access to many of life's pleasures, including possessions, experiences, and gifts to worthy causes. On the flipside, its mismanagement has ruined many lives and families and is routinely among the top reasons for divorce and suicide. For these, and many other reasons, it's critical that you become a wise manager of your financial resources. Money represents the fruit of your labor and provision from God, and you should treat it with diligence, respect, and good stewardship. Remember that God owns it all (Psalm 24:1), and we are to be both prudent and generous with the resources and gifts He's given us.

Surprisingly, you needn't be a rocket scientist to effectively manage your finances well. Yet, many people are intimidated by the thought. For the most part, the principles of wise financial management aren't that tough to master. You simply need to know the basics and abide by sound disciplines and principles.

People who are wise financial managers have several advantages in life. One is their stress levels are much lower than folks who live paycheck to paycheck. Second, it enables them to save up for major purchases (e.g., college, a second home, vacation of a lifetime) and support a good retirement. Third, it allows people to meaningfully contribute to worthy, charitable causes to help the broader community.

When it comes to managing your finances, there are really only three things you have to master. One is learning how to live within your means (i.e., not spending more than you earn). Another is knowing how to patiently build wealth in order to achieve your goals. The third is having a successful career and avoiding the poverty drivers you learned about in Chapter Nine of the book. If you achieve these three objectives and become financially literate, you'll be well-positioned to manage your finances.

Finally, it pays to understand (and commit to avoiding) the most common financial mistakes people make:

1. Failure to set goals and plan for major purchases and retirement
2. Spending more than they earn and failing to budget and monitor expenses
3. Incurring too much debt, including excessive credit card usage
4. Investing too little and starting too late
5. Incurring significant fixed expenses that can't be reduced in difficult economic times (e.g., spending too much on housing and cars)
6. Ill-timed investment decisions ("buy high, sell low" habits and market timing)
7. Poorly diversified investment portfolios (overly concentrated in high-risk stocks)
8. Impulse buying and lack of value consciousness when shopping
9. Inadequate financial knowledge
10. Lack of discipline and personal responsibility

OBJECTIVES:

▌ Learn the five key elements of wise financial management
▌ Practice living within your financial means by monitoring spending and generating positive cash flow
▌ Commit to using credit sparingly and wisely to avoid the debt trap
▌ Develop the discipline of planning for your short- and long-term goals
▌ Learn the benefits of investing early, regularly, and as much as you can in a disciplined, long-term strategy
▌ Appreciate the virtue of patience when building your long-term wealth

 Prepare

▌ **Read Chapter 10 ("Managing Your Finances") in *What I Wish I Knew at 18*, starting on page 209.**
▌ **Use your highlighter pen to highlight anything in the chapter that jumps out at you—things you want to remember, take note of, come back to, or discuss later.**
▌ **In the chart below, identify the pointers that meet the following criteria:**

1. the most important in life
2. ones you think you are already doing well and can model to others
3. ones you either find the most challenging or in which you may need guidance to apply to your life

1. the most important in life

2. ones you think you are already doing well and can model to others

3. ones you either find the most challenging or in which you may need guidance to apply to your life

POINTER #1 — STRIVE TO BECOME A WISE STEWARD, DISCIPLINED SAVER, PRUDENT CONSUMER, CAUTIOUS DEBTOR, AND CHEERFUL GIVER

 Consider

For many, the subject of money management is intimidating and even overwhelming. After all, there's a lot to learn, including a new vocabulary that's riddled with jargon. So, let's begin with the basics and first define the target. Here's what it will look like when you become a successful manager of your finances:

- *A Wise Steward*—one who understands the key aspects of money and finance and who manages his resources in a sound, disciplined, and principled manner (see Matthew 25:14–21)
- *A Disciplined Saver*—one who saves and invests on a regular basis and lives within means in order to save for the future (see Proverbs 6:6–11, 27:12)
- *A Prudent Consumer*—one who has a keen understanding of "value" and who spends money conservatively and wisely, rather than impulsively (see Proverbs 31:16–18)
- *A Cautious Debtor*—one who uses debt sparingly and who saves in order to fund major purchases (see Romans 13:7–8)
- *A Cheerful Giver*—one who gives generously to causes that benefit the community and the world (see 1 Timothy 6:18)

Keep these qualities in mind both now and in the future as your earnings evolve. Periodically review how you're doing in each of these five areas. If you can successfully achieve these goals, you'll be in excellent financial shape and allow your generosity to impact the world.

You CAN learn to be a successful manager of your finances!

Discuss

In your small group, discuss the following questions (some may include activities to do together). Be honest and respect others' responses. There are no right or wrong answers and your group should be a safe place to talk and share freely.

Consider the above qualities of wise financial management and talk about:

▌ Which principles you believe you already understand and can easily adopt in your life
▌ Which will be the most challenging for you, knowing your current habits and financial understanding
▌ Why, in your opinion, most people struggle at managing their finances (and what you can do to avoid their mistakes!)
▌ Some things you think would help you, at your age and season of life, get a head start on good financial management

Apply

1. Take the time to record some steps you can take to help become a wise financial manager. Use the Journal section at the end of the chapter to record your ideas. Include ways you can improve your knowledge and habits.
2. Interview your parent(s) regarding the five qualities of successful financial managers and have them conduct a self-evaluation. Do they have suggestions for how you can improve in the area(s) that are most challenging for you? What do they wish they would have done differently in managing their finances?

Words to Live By

Know the state of your flocks, and put your heart into caring for your herds. —Proverbs 27:23

POINTER #2 —
LIVE WITHIN YOUR MEANS AND GENERATE POSITIVE CASH FLOW/CREATE REGULAR CASH FLOW STATEMENTS AND ANALYZE YOUR SPENDING/USE CREDIT SPARINGLY AND WISELY

 Consider

When it comes to managing money, one of the toughest challenges is that there are so many things to do with it! For this reason, and the widespread availability of credit, it's easy for people to lose control. This is why it takes great discipline and restraint to manage our money well.

The fact is that everyone is in a different financial situation. That's because we choose different careers with wildly varying pay, live in different places, have different family sizes, and have different habits and desires. If that isn't enough, we have peers and neighbors with fancier possessions that can be awfully tempting. Interestingly, people with high incomes can run into financial problems just like folks with more modest incomes. It's just that the things they spend money on are more expensive!

Regardless of your income, it's essential to have the discipline of spending less than you earn (in order to generate "positive cash flow") and have enough left over to save and invest for your future. **That means automatically investing first and living on the rest rather than spending first and investing what's left.** It also means closely monitoring your spending by creating cash flow statements (that detail your income and spending on various items) and avoiding the overuse of credit cards to pay for your daily expenses. The availability of credit has led to chronic overspending and financial problems for many people when they are unable to pay off their monthly balances.

It's essential to spend less than you earn!

The greater the debt, the more difficult it is to handle tougher economic times. The best way to control debt is by not using it pay for things you really can't afford. The "buy now-pay later" mentality is a trap that will only dig a financial hole that can be very difficult to climb out of. For this reason, the Bible warns us, "Just as the rich rule the poor, so the borrower is servant to the lender" (Proverbs 22:7). Obviously, loans like mortgages and car loans are a practical necessity in our culture. But credit card debt that you cannot pay off each month will only spiral into financial disaster that will rob your peace of mind and prevent you from using your God-given provision for its intended purposes.

So, the secret to managing your daily finances is to spend less than you earn (which allows you to invest for the future), monitor your spending (considering the percentages included in the back of this book), use credit and loans sparingly (to pay off your full balance each month), and being a prudent consumer who understands the difference between needs and wants. Whether your career is lucrative or modest, if you do these things well, you'll be in good shape.

Discuss

1. Complete together, as a group, the "(Sort of) Real World Budgeting Exercise" in the Appendix on page 161–162.
2. In your small group, discuss the advantages of:

▌ Spending less than you earn and saving and investing the rest
▌ Monitoring your spending through the use of a cash flow statement (see example on page 163 of Appendix)
▌ Using credit sparingly and not spending on what you cannot afford

Are you prepared to commit to doing these three things when managing your budget? What will be the most challenging for you?

Apply

Throughout your life, it's critical that you monitor your spending to ensure you're living within your means. One component of this is a cash flow statement (sample on page 163), which details how you distribute your income to spending, savings, and charitable giving. This will help you identify how you are spending your money in different areas.

The next step is to develop a budget, which compares your *actual* spending to your *budgeted* (or targeted) level of spending. You will first need to develop spending targets for different expense categories (e.g., housing, food,) and then compare your actual spending to these amounts. Your goal is to spend less than you budget. Further explanation and blank budget worksheets appear on pages 164 to 166 in the Appendix section of this study guide. You can use these worksheets throughout your life and, if you already have income, start now.

Words to Live By

If you are faithful in little things, you will be faithful in large ones. But if you are dishonest in little things, you won't be honest with greater responsibilities. And if you are untrustworthy about worldly wealth, who will trust you with the true riches of heaven? —Jesus, in Luke 16:10–11

POINTER #3 —
DEVELOP A FINANCIAL PLAN THAT REFLECTS YOUR SHORT- AND LONG-TERM GOALS

 Consider

Are you a goal setter? If you are, and you're a diligent planner and implementer, you're probably a pretty successful person!

Goal setting is critically important in the area of finances. You'll find that many of your goals involve substantial sums of money, and it takes planning to reach them. Among the most common financial-related goals are your: 1) education, 2) car, 3) down payment on your home, 4) children's education, and 5) retirement. Some of these goals will come soon (short-term), some will be in the next 5–10 years (intermediate-term), and some are much further down the road (long-term).

For each of these goals, you need to develop a financial plan that gets you there and determine how much you'll need to save and invest for each goal. For the longer range goals, where you have ample time to grow your assets, develop a long-term investment program to build your nest egg. Your assets will grow as a result of the money you contribute and the rate of return you earn on your investments.

You'll reach your goals sooner and more cost effectively if you become a dedicated planner, saver, and investor. What's not to like about that?

 Discuss

1. Many people fail to take into account their need to save and invest each month to reach their goals. Why is this the case? When you look ahead over the next 20 years, which things do you think you'll need to save up for in your life? How will you make room for them when there are so many things you may want to buy NOW?

2. Consulting Exercise: Complete, as a group, the "You're the Financial Advisor" exercise on page 167 of the Appendix at the back of your student guide. You will become the consultants to the "Spendthrift" family. Use what you've learned to analyze their financial situation, help them develop a cash flow statement and budget, and make some recommendations for lifestyle adjustments to help them live within their budget.

Apply

To help you become a good financial planner, consider items requiring major spending over the next 1 to 5, 5 to 10, 20 to 30, and over 30 years. Then, come up with an estimate of how much money you'll need for each item. Finally, take the total for each item and divide it by the number of years you'll need to save for it and calculate the amount of savings you'll need per year for each goal. It adds up, doesn't it? By doing this exercise beforehand, it will reinforce the importance of not spending all of your earnings on items you want *now*. Good planning requires the discipline of putting off spending now for the sake of important items you'll need later.

POINTER #4 —
INVEST EARLY, REGULARLY, AND AS MUCH AS YOU CAN IN A DIVERSIFIED, LONG-TERM STRATEGY

Consider

In order to achieve your long-term goals and maintain your lifestyle in retirement, you'll need to build financial wealth. How much your money eventually grows will be a function of the following:

1. How much you invest (more is better!)
2. The rate of return on your investments (higher is better!)
3. The time period over which you are investing (longer is better!)

Your chances of accumulating significant wealth will be greater if you invest as much as you can as early in your career as you can. Many people struggle at this because there are so many things to buy in the first 10 years after high school!

One of the best ways to do this is to have an automatic investment plan that takes money from your bank account on a monthly basis and invests it in a diversified investment program according to your desired level of risk.

How early in your life you begin investing has a more significant impact on your wealth than you can possibly imagine. This is because of the power of compounding your returns over many years. For example, if you had a $5,000 investment that grew at 6% per year over 40 years it would increase to $51,429 (a 10-bagger!). However, if you waited 20 years to start, that same initial $5,000 would only grow to $16,036. Are you ready for a shocker? If your $5,000 investment grew instead by 10% per year, it would be worth $226,297 after 40 years compared with $33,637 after 20 years! Now, you can see why so many people will never have enough money saved for retirement if they wait too long to get started! And, why it pays to generate strong rates of return on your investments. It also pays to avoid trying to time the market (move your money in and out of stocks based on your view of the market)—nobody does this well on a consistent basis.

Beginning your investment program as soon as you start your career should be a top priority. Save and invest early, regularly, and as much as you can in a diversified, long-term investment program. It will provide you with the best chances of building significant wealth for your retirement, achieving financial freedom, and giving generously to charitable causes.

THINK ABOUT THIS!

Let's assume you start investing on a monthly basis and earn a 6% annualized rate of return until your retirement at age 65. If your goal is to have accumulated $1 million at retirement and you start at age 23 you will reach that target if you invest $441 per month (a little over $100/ week). Are you surprised? But, let's say you're late to the game (as most are) and start 20 years later (age 43). Guess how much you have to invest per month to reach $1 million by 65? Try $1,831/month or roughly $460 per week! That's a lot of catching up to do!

Discuss

In your small group discuss the following:

▌ What are the advantages of investing as soon as you can and doing what you need to do to make room for investing in your budget? Would you be more likely to do this if you automatically invested each month?

▌ Were you surprised at how much more your money grows over long periods and the impact that higher rates of return have on your wealth? Knowing this, is it possible to be too conservative with your investments?

▌ Given the fact that it is impossible to consistently predict the direction of the stock market, why do so many try? When the market declines, will you have the courage to stick it out? To buy more at lower prices?

▌ If you could own one stock, what would it be and why?

Apply

Start familiarizing yourself with the financial markets. Learn about stocks (an ownership position in a public company), bonds (longer-term loans that pay interest), mutual funds (pools of money invested in different securities for multiple shareholders), and the economy. Start reading the business news section of your paper/websites and watch financial networks (e.g., CNBC, FoxBusiness, and Bloomberg). Think of some different companies you'd like to invest in and build a "paper portfolio" to see how it would perform. Watch them rise and fall from day to day to acquaint yourself with how the markets move. Be SKEPTICAL of anyone claiming that they know how to predict the market. Think long term! Finally, as soon as you begin your career, if not sooner, start investing on a monthly basis. Time is on your side!

POINTER #5 — GROW YOUR WEALTH PATIENTLY

Consider

In life, patience is a virtue. In investing, it's an absolute necessity! Inexperienced investors often fall for get rich quick schemes and hot stock tips. They buy at the top, *after* the big gains already happened and just before the stock plunges. They sell at the bottom when times are scary (but when the values are best). Most people simply don't understand that you can't predict future performance from the past and it costs them dearly.

As mentioned previously, your best bet is to regularly invest in a diversified, long-term strategy (that includes stocks and bonds) rather than engage in market timing. The tendency for most investors is to speculate (take too much risk) at the top of the market when prices are high and capitulate (panic sell) at the market bottom after they've lost a ton of money. It's the opposite of "buy low, sell high," and it's a wealth destroyer. The average investor loses around 2% per year because of lousy timing.

Wealth from get-rich-quick schemes quickly disappears; wealth from **hard work** grows over time

—Proverbs 13:11

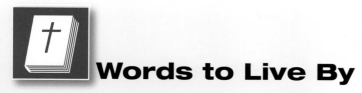

Words to Live By

But divide your investments among many places, for you do not know what risks might lie ahead.
—Ecclesiastes 11:2

Another key investment principle is to avoid overly concentrating your investments in a few stocks or market segments (e.g., technology). Your wealth will be too dependent upon the returns of a few investments, and it's a risk that is simply not worth taking. As a rule of thumb, no stock should represent more than 10–15% of your assets. You want to diversify across different investments in order to have steadier returns.

The power of diversification is illustrated in the following chart. **Recall, your goal is to grow your wealth *steadily*.** If you chose to invest in only investment A or B, your wealth would be on quite a roller coaster ride! But, did you notice how investments A and B move in opposite (complementary) directions? This means they are good "diversifiers" to each other because when one falls, the other rises.

Good examples of diversifiers are oil and airline stocks because one is helped when oil prices rise while the other is hurt. The wise choice is to own both investments A and B (depicted by path C) because they complement each other well and offer a much smoother ride over time. It's best to save the roller coasters for the amusement park!

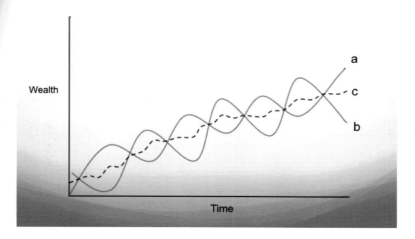

Diversification in a Picture

Remember that one of the key requirements to building wealth is avoiding major losses.

Finally, be sure to invest in both stocks and bonds. Even though bonds offer lower long-term returns, they provide stability and great diversification when the stock market declines.

Discuss

In your small group, discuss the following questions:

▌ Have you ever considered investing? Why or why not?

▌ Do you know people who invest regularly? Do you think this influenced your answer to the previous question?

▌ How will you react in your investing when the stock market has big gains or large losses? Will you have the courage to sell after a big increase and buy after a big loss?

▌ Why is it that just because a stock was a good investment last year, it may not continue to be?

▌ What are some examples of different investments that are good "diversifiers" to each other (i.e., when one falls, the other rises)?

Above and Beyond

Here's a brief Bible study you can do to help improve your understanding about God's perspective (and instructions) on handling finances. Look up the following verses and note what each says about money and how we are to regard it. The answers can be found in the Appendix on page 171.

SCRIPTURE	FINANCIAL PRINCIPLE
Deuteronomy 8:18	
Psalm 24:1	
Psalm 37:21	
Proverbs 3:9–10	
Proverbs 22:7	
Ecclesiastes 11:2	
Matthew 6:24	
Luke 12:15	
Luke 19:12–27	
Acts 20:35	
Romans 13:7–8	
Philippians 4:11–13	
1 Timothy 6:6–8	

Apply

To be a successful long-term investor, you need to have steady growth in your investments and avoid major losses. This is because the impact of large losses is so significant. To understand this, complete the following table (columns two and four) assuming a $5,000 investment that has two very different back-to-back years. The formula to use is:

$$\text{beginning investment} \times [1 + \text{return (in decimals)}] = \text{ending value}$$

Year 1 Return	End of Year 1 Value	Year 2 Return	End of Year 2 Value
10%	$5,500	-10%	_____
20%	_____	-20%	_____
50%	_____	-50%	_____

Most people think you add the returns in the rows (which total 0) so it doesn't matter. However, notice the significant differences in the values at the end of Year 2 for each row. It clearly shows that large losses have a much larger impact than small losses. This is why we diversify our investments!

You can use the spaces below to record your thoughts, ideas, and reflections from your personal prayer times as you work through the section on "Managing Your Finances."

OUTCOMES OF THIS SECTION

After this section on "Managing Your Finances," you should be able to:

▍ Understand the major financial mistakes to avoid
▍ Recognize the qualities of wise financial management
▍ Learn how to live within your financial means and monitor your spending with a cash flow statement and budget
▍ Understand the pitfalls of excessive debt and credit card usage
▍ Develop short-, intermediate-, and long-term financial goals
▍ Understand the benefits of investing early, regularly, and as much as you can in a diversified, long-term strategy
▍ Learn to patiently build your wealth by being properly diversified and avoiding large losses

Continue to reflect on the other pointers you read in this chapter of the book, *What I Wish I Knew at 18,* which may not be included in this student manual. The "Take Five" sections are especially helpful to gauge how that particular pointer might be of help or encouragement to you. Don't skip them . . . they may just turn out to be the best part!

Chapter 9 — SPIRITUAL LIFE AND HANDLING ADVERSITY

Adversity

Accept that adversity is a part of life * *Adversity can be preparation for greater things and often makes sense in retrospect* * Day follows night * *Release your pain* * Take seemingly insurmountable challenges one step at a time * **Take charge of your worries** * Don't make an important decision while you're upset—sleep on it * Seek opportunities to help others in even worse shape*

Spirituality

Invest in your spiritual growth * Seek God's wisdom in matters big and small * Count your blessings * **Reserve time for daily reflection and prayer** * Be a wise steward and cheerful giver * **Connect with a worship family** * **Develop an accountability relationship with a trusted friend** * Keep the faith during times of trial*

"Some things have to be **believed** to be **seen**."
—Ralph Hodgson

> *Now faith is confidence in what we hope for and assurance about what we do not see. —Hebrews 11:1*

Cultivating Your Spiritual Life

Humans are, by their very nature, spiritual beings. From the beginning of human history, there is evidence that people have tried to connect another realm, confirming what the Bible has said all along: "He has set eternity in the hearts of men" (Ecclesiastes 3:11). Indeed, surveys routinely indicate that 80–90% of people believe in God and Heaven, in one way or another.

The Bible teaches us that the world we live in does, indeed, have two realms—a physical realm and a spiritual realm. "Set your sights on the *realities of heaven*," the apostle Paul wrote. "Let heaven fill your thoughts. Do not think only about things down here on earth" (Colossians 3:1–2). In the physical realm—the one we see on a daily basis—we navigate by our five natural senses. We see, we hear, we smell, we taste, and we touch. In the spiritual realm, however, our physical senses do us little good. We need to learn to "walk by the Spirit," the Bible tells us (Galatians 5:25). We need to cultivate our spiritual life—and we do it by exercising and growing in our faith.

What's involved in having a meaningful spiritual life? People of the Christian faith often describe their spiritual walk as offering:

▌ A dynamic personal relationship with God through Jesus Christ
▌ Answers to questions of an eternal nature
▌ A place to turn with their gratitude, praises, and needs

▌ A guide to their daily living, a moral compass, and a source of accountability

▌ A means to cleanse the spirit through confession and repentance

▌ A unique community of like-minded believers

▌ A sense of security, purpose, and significance

▌ Comfort and hope in the midst of uncertainty and anguish

Handling Adversity

One of the strongest benefits of a life of faith is the comfort and hope it offers during our most difficult times. Everyone starts out on a journey—any kind of journey—with great expectations. No doubt as you're getting ready to start on your own life journey as an adult, you, too, have hopes and dreams about what the future will look like. We all do, and rightly so.

It would not be realistic, however, to expect a straight line to your dreams and that you won't face trials and opposition. The fact is, you WILL experience adversity at some time or another—it's simply a fact of life. But how you face these defining moments makes all the difference in the world.

Adversity can come in many forms, such as personal loss, disappointments, mistakes, bad luck, and mistreatment. It can affect you physically or mentally or both. In some cases, you may be prepared for it, but in other situations it will appear to come out of the blue when you least expect it.

How will *you* handle adversity? Will you become depressed or take it in stride? Will you become hopeless or look for solutions? Will you be bitter in the wake of an injustice, or will you forgive and move on? Will you trust God for the outcome and continue to serve Him even when you don't understand what's happening to you?

As a young adult, it's important that you develop personal strategies for coping with and overcoming adversity. If your parents have taught you this, all the better; you have role models to follow. If those around you haven't handled it well, don't be discouraged. No matter what your genetics, circumstances, temperament, or personality might be, you can learn how to face adversity and allow it to positively shape your character. After all, adversity can be important preparation for great accomplishments to come or a catalyst to move in a new and better direction. You just never know!

OBJECTIVES:

▌ Recognize the value of investing in your spiritual growth and setting aside regular time for reflection and prayer

▌ Learn to seek God for His wisdom and direction in matters big and small

▌ Recognize the value and importance of connecting with a church family and developing an accountability relationship with a trusted friend(s)

▌ Recognize that adversity happens to everyone; it's part of life

▌ Understand how adversity can strengthen your character and prepare you for other opportunities

▌ Learn strategies for releasing your pain and taking charge of your worries

Prepare

▌ Read Chapters Four ("Spiritual Life," page 101) and Five ("Handling Adversity," page 113) in *What I Wish I Knew at 18*.

▌ Use your highlighter pen to highlight anything in the chapters that jumps out at you—things you want to remember, take note of, come back to, or discuss later.

▌ In the chart below, identify the pointers that meet the following criteria:

    1. the most important in life
    2. ones you think you are already doing well and can model to others
    3. ones you either find the most challenging or in which you may need guidance to apply to your life

1. the most important in life

2. ones you think you are already doing well and can model to others

3. ones you either find the most challenging or in which you may need guidance to apply to your life

POINTER #1 —
INVEST IN YOUR SPIRITUAL GROWTH/
RESERVE TIME FOR DAILY REFLECTION
AND PRAYER

 Consider

Just as our career and relationships demand continual investment, so it is with our spiritual life. Yet, when we are at our busiest, it seems that our spiritual life often takes a backseat. People with active spiritual lives are committed and take a holistic approach through involvement in the following areas:

▌ Personal devotions, meditation, prayer, and reflection
▌ Scripture reading
▌ Worship services
▌ Fellowship groups
▌ Classes
▌ Ministerial services, mission trips, and community outreach opportunities

Here's a big heads-up: Be sure you keep up the momentum after high school! Leaving home—college and beyond—is a time of newfound freedom and, along with it, many potential distractions. You may have a total blast! You may also get a bit overwhelmed by what's going on around you. In many cases the whole secular scene, the opportunities for partying, etc., may lead you down a very wrong road. And all that comes at a time when you may be on your own in a new town. You may need to find a new worship place, which can be a daunting task.

You'll have to be the one to decide to carve out time for your spiritual life. *You'll* have to make the commitment to stand firm in your relationship with God. Don't be one who checks out on your

faith walk when you check into college. This is a time in your life when you need Him more than ever for direction, courage, strength, and upholding your values.

Don't be one who checks out on your faith walk when you check into college.

The bottom line is that if you have faith and desire a rich spiritual life, you have to make room for it. Otherwise, it'll simply get squeezed out by the busyness of life. That's why taking time daily for personal spiritual enrichment and reflection really helps.

Choose some reading material that will help you grow, whether it's Scripture reading that pertains to your faith or perhaps a book of devotions, meditations, or an inspiring biography of someone else's faith walk. Put it by your bed or somewhere else you'll see it (and use it) daily. We need to take time to read as well as express our gratitude, needs, and confessions. Daily reflection time not only promotes our spiritual growth; it also provides balance and perspective. Don't just give it your leftovers. Rather, consider it a gift to yourself as part of your spiritual foundation.

And don't forget the importance of having a regular prayer life. The Christian faith is not simply a collection of principles by which to live. It is a living, dynamic relationship with a living Person. God is a Father who loves to communicate with His children.

If you're not sure how to pray, don't worry; you're not alone. Jesus' own disciples had the same problem! We see the disciples asking Jesus to teach them to pray, specifically, in Matthew 6 and Luke 11, where Jesus gave them the Lord's Prayer. But communicating with God is more than just repeating a rote prayer. Later in the Luke 11 passage, Jesus pointed out to His disciples that God wants us to relate to Him as we would a close friend. We can come to Him any time, even when we would never dare go to someone else. We can be persistent and bold because of our friendship with Him. We can initiate. We can presume. We can even border on bugging Him! Jesus said, "No longer do I call you slaves, for the slave does not know what his master is doing; *but I have called you friends . . .*" (John 15:15, emphasis added).

Too often we come knocking when we want something. Yes, God delights to meet our needs but He offers (and desires) so much more than that. He is a Person with a heart, feelings, longings, understanding and insight, wisdom, and affection that He wants to share with His children and friends—including you!

Discuss

Are you allowing room in your life for spiritual growth? For Bible reading and personal reflection? For prayer? When reviewing the above list of spiritual growth avenues, are there areas that would be especially interesting or helpful to you? Share with your small group any of these that you practice regularly, and how they have impacted you.

Then brainstorm some strategies for maintaining your faith walk and connecting with other Christians (and a new church) when you leave high school and home. What are some ways you can keep up your spiritual momentum?

Words to Live By

But Jesus told him, "No! The Scriptures say, 'People do not live by bread alone, but by every word that comes from the mouth of God.'" —Matthew 4:4

"My heart has heard you say, 'Come and talk with me.' And my heart responds, 'Lord, I am coming.'" —Psalm 27:8

Apply

Develop a system to help you read the Bible regularly and systematically. Consider asking a friend to join you so you can encourage one another and discuss questions and insights. There are a number of good "read-through-the-Bible-in-a-year" models and other similar Scripture reading programs available. Read carefully and prayerfully. The Bible is more than just a book you'd read like any other. Ask God to speak to you as you read, and to make His word come alive to you. Don't just ask, "What does this mean?" Ask, "What does this mean *for me*?"

Above and Beyond

Check out the following Scriptures that describe Jesus' own prayer life: Luke 5:16, 6:12, 12:37, 22:39–40. Jesus' life was every bit as chaotic and pressured as ours is, even more so. He left us a wonderful, powerful example of a life of prayer that fueled a life of love, compassion, and supernatural power. What can you observe from Jesus' habits and patterns of spending time with God? How can you apply what you learn to your own spiritual life?

POINTER #2 —
SEEK GOD'S WISDOM IN MATTERS BIG AND SMALL

Consider

Think about how amazing Jesus' life was. He did miracles. He healed people. He was full of wisdom and power. But what's really amazing is that as a flesh and blood human being, Jesus did nothing of His own initiative. He only acted as He received instruction and power from the Father by the Holy Spirit (see John 5:30, 8:28, 42, 12:49, 14:10).

You may think, "I'm not as important as Jesus. Why should I expect to hear from God? I shouldn't bother Him with my little problems." That would not be the case! You are important to God. Everything about you is important to Him, from the big things to the small things. Jesus wanted us to do the things that He did, to seek out and hear from God the way He did, and to do the kinds of things He did (John 14:12). And He wanted us to *pray* the way He did, because it was in the times of prayer with the Father that He received instruction, strength, and the Holy Spirit's power.

You have many decisions ahead of you. *You'll need wisdom.* You will experience many circumstances that will test your endurance. *You'll need strength.* You will have many opportunities that present themselves for the taking. *You'll need direction.* All these are reason enough to start the practice of seeking God regularly for His wisdom, strength, and direction, no matter how big (or small) the situation. Sometimes it's His answer to little prayers where He is most evident—in those situations where they simply couldn't have happened by chance.

 **Discuss**

"Lord, listening is one of the hardest things we ever try to do and few people do it well. But, Lord, You listen to us and You call us by name when You answer. Thank You for the privilege we have to be like children and come bounding into Your presence. Help us to be quiet and listen while You share Your ideas, dreams, and love with us. We want to hear everything You have to tell us." —Charles Wesley, English hymn writer and church leader, 1707–1788

Read and discuss the quote above from Charles Wesley, who wrote and published over 6,000 hymns—many of which are still sung in churches today. It's interesting to note how heavily he depended on "listening" for God's voice and direction. What are some times you know *you've* had a clear sense or impression from God when you asked for His help or wisdom? Share these in your small group.

 **Apply**

Start a prayer journal in which you record what you're praying about, the date you started praying, and what you sense God saying to you about that situation (see example below). Also record answers you receive to specific prayers, and the date and way in which they were answered.

Don't be discouraged if you don't have immediate answers or responses to record. Keep this record for the long run. It will eventually start to fill up! Many people find such a journal to be a great encouragement and faith builder over the long haul.

Date	Prayer Request	Impressions	Answer/Date

POINTER #3 —
CONNECT WITH A WORSHIP FAMILY AND DEVELOP AN ACCOUNTABILITY RELATIONSHIP WITH A TRUSTED FRIEND

 Consider

Chances are, if you've attended some sort of worship services at all in your life, you've gone with your parents. However, since many high school grads eventually relocate or may have different preferences than their parents, you may find yourself looking for a new venue for practicing and growing in your faith. Fortunately, most communities and colleges offer a wide range of choices, including spiritually-focused organizations for young adults.

If you're committed to your spiritual growth, it's important to connect with a worship center of some kind. It will offer opportunities for fellowship, service, and education. Even if it hasn't been important to you up until now, seeking out a faith/worship venue can be very beneficial to you. It can even boost your GPA! That's right. Students who attend religious services weekly average a GPA 0.144 higher than those who never attend services, said Jennifer Glanville, a sociologist at the University of Iowa. And researchers found that church attendance had even more impact on a teen's GPA than whether or not the parents earned a college degree. High school students who went to church weekly also had lower dropout rates and felt more a part of their schools.

Why is that? For one, according to this study, students who regularly attend a faith/worship center have regular contact with older adults from various generations who serve as role models and mentors. Another is that they more easily and readily develop friendships with peers who have similar norms and values.[8]

That brings up another key point in your spiritual development. It's very helpful to find a trusted confidante (of your own gender) with whom you can share your innermost feelings and who has your best interests at heart. It should be someone who will both encourage you and hold you accountable when your spiritual life, relationships, or actions get off track; someone with whom you can connect and pray with and for each other on a regular basis. Granted, it takes time and effort to build a trusted friendship of that caliber, but it'll be hugely beneficial to you. Objective and sometimes critical, feedback from someone you respect and who cares deeply about you is valuable. It may even be one of the ways God chooses to speak to you from time to time.

 Words to Live By

As iron sharpens iron, so a friend sharpens a friend. —Proverbs 27:7

 Discuss

This section lists several benefits of involvement with a worship family of some sort. What are they? Can you think of others? What about the benefits of being involved with a Christian organization of people your own age? Can you think of any? Share your ideas and experiences with the group. (Note: Remember that everyone's thoughts may be different. Be polite and respectful of other people's perspectives.)

 **Apply**

Do you plan to avail yourself of worship and fellowship opportunities when you leave home after high school? *It should be one of your highest priorities.* If you're currently in college, have you checked out the fellowship and ministry opportunities on your campus? Have you learned (in this chapter and in others throughout this course) the importance and benefits of connecting with people of similar values for support and friendship?

> *If you have faith and desire a rich spiritual life you have to make room for it.*

When the time comes, take the time to "shop around" for a worship family or Christian fellowship group. Look for one that is compatible with your beliefs, challenges you to grow in your faith and understanding, provides educational opportunities, offers encouragement, and allows you to build healthy, supportive, and accountable friendships.

POINTER #4 —
ACCEPT THAT ADVERSITY IS PART OF LIFE—IT CAN BE PREPARATION FOR GREATER THINGS AND OFTEN MAKES SENSE IN RETROSPECT

 Consider

> *Therefore, since we are surrounded by such a huge crowd of witnesses to the life of faith, let us strip off every weight that slows us down, especially the sin that so easily trips us up. And let us run with endurance the race God has set before us. We do this by keeping our eyes on Jesus, the champion who initiates and perfects our faith. Because of the joy awaiting him, he endured the cross, disregarding its shame. Now he is seated in the place of honor beside God's throne. —Hebrews 12:1–2*

In order to succeed in life, you must be able to accept adversity as part of your journey and remember that you're *not* alone when it happens. In some cases, our adversity is self-inflicted, while other times it comes from sources we simply can't control. It's also important to accept that your adversity isn't some "payback" for something you've previously done. It just happens—to everyone— as a part of life.

One of life's greatest adventures is seeing what becomes of our trials. At our bleakest hour, it's hard to fathom that something good might come of our woes. Often, though, this is precisely what happens, particularly when we have eventual opportunities to come alongside others who are going through the same thing. The empathy and perspective we can offer others is that much more powerful when we have endured similar trials.

"You may not realize it when it happens, but a kick in the teeth may be the best thing in the world for you."
—Walt Disney

When you're experiencing a personal trial, consider that it might be preparation for something greater or that it is a catalyst for going in a different, and better, direction. After all, often our greatest character growth comes from enduring life's greatest challenges. The Bible tells us, "We can rejoice, too, when we run into problems and trials, for we know that they help us develop endurance. And endurance develops strength of character, and character strengthens our confident hope of salvation" (Romans 5:3–4). You've no doubt heard the saying in athletics, "No pain, no gain." The same is true of character building. Muscle is one of the only (if not THE only) machines that gets better and stronger the longer and more often you use it. In a similar way, we build solid character through meeting, navigating, and overcoming the challenges and disappointments life throws at us.

Discuss

In your small group, discuss the following questions (some may include activities to do together). Be honest and respect others' responses. There are no right or wrong answers and your group should be a safe place to talk and share freely.

1. Consider some of the major life trials you've experienced. Are you able to see some good that came out of those periods? How were you aware of God's help and comfort in the midst of it? How was your character affected by it? What strengths did you need to call on within yourself (or from God) to deal with it—and what new strengths do you think the adversity developed in you?
2. Can you think of people you know who have experienced significant adversity? How has it shaped them for the better?
3. Have you been able to come alongside another who is going through tough times and been able to offer wise advice or prayerful encouragement and support because of your own experience? Tell about it.

Words to Live By

He comforts us in all our troubles so that we can comfort others. When they are troubled, we will be able to give them the same comfort God has given us. —2 Corinthians 1:4

Apply

Turn to the Values exercise you completed in Chapter Two (page 25). Using your highlighter pen, mark the values you think have been strengthened in you because of difficult circumstances you've had to go through. Does it help you realize that the adversity you faced had some positive results in your life and character development?

POINTER #5 —
RELEASE YOUR PAIN/TAKE CHARGE OF YOUR WORRIES

Consider

When we're going through a difficult time, we often take lousy care of ourselves. Some people overeat out of stress. Some people stop eating altogether. Some don't sleep well. Some may bottle up their feelings and hibernate; others tell anyone who will listen. Some fall into a depression. Sometimes people are even tempted to medicate their stress with false comforts like alcohol and drugs.

You need to know there is a better way! In order to deal with your anguish (and preserve your health and peace of mind), tap into your personal stress outlets and release your pain. These might include (and this is not an exhaustive list):

- Praying! Seek out God's wisdom, perspective, and hope.
- Seeking out a support system (of people who can really give you good advice). Look both inside AND outside of your peer group. Don't be afraid to ask for help.
- Finding something creative or productive to do
- Sleeping and eating well, even if you don't feel like it
- Exercising
- Helping someone less fortunate than yourself. This often helps put your own problems into perspective and show you it's not as bad as you may think.

Don't Worry!

This could have been a point on the above list, but it's worth a section of its own. Whether or not you choose to worry can make or break you. Have you ever noticed that some people are chronic worriers while others take things in stride? Most people who worry are simply thoughtful people who tend to think too long and hard on the wrong things. Worry is always motivated by fear, and fear saps us of energy and joy. Life is too short to worry all the time!

If you happen to be the worrying type, ponder the following questions:

"**Worry** never robs **tomorrow** of its **sorrow**, it only saps **today** of its **joy.**"
—Leo Buscaglia

- In the end, how often have your worries been justified?
- If things didn't work out, did you still deal with them well?
- Can you remember what you were worried about a year ago?
- What do you tend to worry about and why?
- What is the underlying fear behind the worry?
- If you're worried, how can you channel it instead into a productive plan?

Then consider the following suggestions:

- "Don't sweat the small stuff." This is actually a book title, as well as a famous saying. It's true!
- Recognize that your worries alone won't help solve the problem.
- Understand that, generally speaking, things tend to work out fine anyway—and even when they don't, you have the capacity to deal with them.
- Learn that the best approach is to focus on the problem and on what you *can* control.

Words to Live By

Don't worry about anything; instead, pray about everything. Tell God what you need, and thank him for all he has done. Then you will experience God's peace, which exceeds anything we can understand. His peace will guard your hearts and minds as you live in Christ Jesus. —Philippians 4:6–8

Discuss

In your small group, discuss the following situation:

You have just experienced a string of unfortunate and disheartening events. Your house was recently broken into and all your electronic equipment was stolen. Your boyfriend or girlfriend, whom you've been dating for nearly a year, just broke up with you. You didn't get into the college of your choice and all your closest friends have already been accepted by theirs and are making plans for their freshman year.

Together, talk about the healthiest and most creative ways you can think of for overcoming the adversity of these circumstances. Write down your ideas and share them with the larger group.

Above and Beyond

Read Matthew 6:25–34 together as a group. Take note of the things Jesus said about worrying. How do you think He would advise and encourage the people in the scenario you just discussed?

Apply

Reflect on your group discussion time and answer these questions:

▮ Did it help to discuss these challenges with a group of friends?
▮ Did hearing the ideas of others in the group help you to think of other ways to overcome adversity?
▮ Which idea(s) would you like to keep in mind for when you encounter a difficult situation (or for a situation you're dealing with now)? Write these down in the Journal section at the end of this chapter.

Journal

You can use the spaces below to record your thoughts, ideas, and reflections from your personal prayer times as you work through the section on "Spiritual Life and Handling Adversity."

OUTCOMES OF THIS SECTION

After this section on "Spiritual Life and Handling Adversity," you should be able to:

▌ Recognize the value of investing in your spiritual growth and commit to setting aside regular time for reflection, Scripture reading, and prayer

▌ Know the value of connecting with a worship family and developing accountability relationships with trusted friends

▌ Get in the habit of seeking God's wisdom in everything, the big things and the small

▌ Recognize that adversity happens to everyone; it's part of life

▌ Understand how adversity can strengthen your character and prepare you for other things

▌ Learn and apply strategies for releasing your pain and taking charge of your worries

Continue to reflect on the other pointers you read in this chapter of the book, *What I Wish I Knew at 18,* which may not be included in this student manual. The "Take Five" sections are especially helpful to gauge how that particular pointer might be of help or encouragement to you. Don't skip them . . . they may just turn out to be the best part!

CONCLUSION

Congratulations on completing the *What I Wish I Knew at 18* course! Now, armed with the biblical wisdom you need and the experience of honorable leaders captured in *What I Wish I Knew at 18*, you can take on the real world with purpose, passion, honor, and integrity. You are ready to use your unique talents, experiences, and relationships to make a positive impact on mankind.

You are ready to find, follow, and fulfill God's call on your life.
You are ready to LEAD.

Every generation faces its challenges and opportunities. Each person has to find his or her way and choose the life he (or she) wants to live. Back in 1971, a time with geopolitical and cultural issues similar to today's, the group Ten Years After recorded a classic song called, "I'd Love to Change the World." After lamenting the many challenges facing society, they broke into the following chorus:

*I'd love to change the world
But I don't know what to do
So I'll leave it up to you.*

You could choose to look at your life this way. Many do. Or, you could do your part to change the world in amazing, wonderful ways.

Which will it be?
We invite *you* to change the world.
With God's Spirit, strength, courage, wisdom, and love in you,
you have the power for your life to make a positive impact on mankind.
The world is waiting—and it's waiting for YOU!

*I pray that from his glorious, unlimited resources
he will empower you with inner strength through his Spirit.
Then Christ will make his home in your hearts as you trust in him.
Your roots will grow down into God's love and keep you strong.
Ephesians 3:16–17*

APPENDICES

VALUES DESCRIPTORS

Personal Values	Social Values
Healthy living	Compassion
Spirituality/ "God-consciousness"	Justice
Self-discipline	Kindness
Fitness	Forgiveness
Punctuality	Grace
Integrity	Flexibility
Commitment	Hospitality
Trustworthiness	Gentleness
Obedience	Righteousness
Courage	Faith
Purity	Patience
Humility	Generosity
Honesty	Gratitude
Cleanliness	Courage
Sense of fun	Perseverance
Thankfulness	Unconditional love
Loyalty	Contentment
Industriousness	Respect
Financial responsibility	Honor
Modesty	Duty
Reliability	Dignity

BUCKET LIST

GOALS

SHORT-TERM	MEDIUM-TERM	LONG-TERM

WEEKLY HOMEWORK AND STUDY PLANNER

Month _____

Subject	Monday	Tuesday	Wednesday	Thursday	Friday	Sat/Sun

DAILY SCHEDULE/TO-DO

Date _____	Date _____
Morning	**Morning**
6:00	6:00
7:00	7:00
8:00	8:00
9:00	9:00
10:00	10:00
11:00	11:00
Afternoon	**Afternoon**
12:00	12:00
1:00	1:00
2:00	2:00
3:00	3:00
4:00	4:00
5:00	5:00
Evening	**Evening**
6:00	6:00
7:00	7:00
8:00	8:00
9:00	9:00
10:00	10:00
11:00	11:00

BE THE ONLY YOU TEST

Answer the following questions based on your study of pages 233–234 from What I Wish I Knew at 18 *(reproduced on page 77) using the rainbow highlighter study method. Compare your answers with the rest of your group, using the text to help you.*

What is "identity theft?"

_____

_____

_____

_____

What are some ways that our lives are not as private as they used to be? Give two examples.

_____

_____

_____

List four causes of stolen identity.

_____

_____

_____

_____

List at least eight precautions you can take to avoid having your identity stolen (extra bonus points for knowing all twelve).

_____

_____

_____

_____

_____

_____

_____

(SORT OF) REAL WORLD BUDGETING EXERCISE

When it comes to budgeting (allocating your income to living expenses, savings and investments, and charitable donations), it pays to prepare monthly/quarterly cash flow statements. These detail how you spent your money and whether or not you're on track. It's important to note that some living expenses are fixed (you can't reduce these payments—things like your rent/mortgage and car loans) and others are variable (you can change how much you spend month to month (clothing and entertainment). Also, some expenses are essentials (must-haves like food and housing) while others are discretionary (nice-to-haves like fine dining, brand-name clothes, unlimited calling/texting plans).

One of the greatest challenges in managing money is first spending on our *needs* before our *wants*. As consumers, we have many choices in how to spend our money. The key is having the discipline to say no to things we can't afford and making wise choices in how we divvy up our income.

The exercise you're about to do will give you an overly simplistic glimpse at what it is like to budget. Your job is to develop three budgets assuming three different levels of income. You choose the level you wish to spend on Essentials (modest, average, or expensive) as well as on Discretionary items listed on the following page. Produce worksheets that list your income, essential expenses, discretionary expenses, savings and investments, and charitable giving.

▌ What are your priorities?
▌ How did your spending change at the lowest and highest levels of income?

INCOME ASSUMPTIONS:

Income	Taxes
$30,000	$2,700
$50,000	$8,000
$80,000	$17,600

ESSENTIAL EXPENSES:

Housing-related:

Modest	$9,000 ($ 750/mo.)
Average	$12,000 ($1,000/mo.)
Expensive	$24,000 ($2,000/mo.)

Food/Clothing/Other Essentials-related:

Modest	$8,000 ($ 667/mo.)
Average	$12,000 ($1,000/mo.)
Expensive	$16,000 ($1,333/mo.)

Automobile (payment/insurance/maintenance):

Old used car:	$1,200 ($100/mo.)
Newer used car	$4,800 ($400/mo.)
New car	$10,800 ($900/mo.)

DISCRETIONARY EXPENSES:

Entertainment: (movies/dinner/sporting events):

1) 2x week (inexpensive)	$2,600 ($50/wk.)
2) 2x week (medium)	$7,800 ($150/wk.)
3) 2x week (expensive)	$15,600 ($300/wk.)
4) 1x week (inexpensive)	$1,300 ($25/wk.)
5) 1x week (medium)	$3,900 ($75/wk.)
6) 1x week (expensive)	$7,800 ($150/wk.)
7) 1x month (inexpensive)	$300 ($25/wk.)
8) 1x month (medium)	$900 ($75/wk.)
9) 1x month (expensive)	$1,800 ($150/wk.)

Vacations: (travel/hotel/food/etc.):

1) Europe	$5,000 one week; $8,000 two weeks
2) Hawaii	$3,500 one week; $6,000 two weeks
3) Southern California	$2,500 one week; $4,000 two weeks
4) RV trip	$1,000 one week; $1,750 two weeks
5) Camping	$300 one week; $500 two weeks

Health Insurance:

Premium Plan	$7,200 ($600/mo.)
Good Plan	$4,500 ($375/mo.)
Basic Plan	$2,400 ($200/mo.)

Cable TV Packages:

Premium (all stations)	$1,200 ($100/mo.)
Average (some extras)	$840 ($ 70/mo.)
Basic	$480 ($ 40/mo.)

Budget Worksheet Guidelines:

▌ Select one level of spending in each Essential and Discretionary category
▌ Assume three weeks of vacation
▌ Remember to save room for investments and charitable giving
▌ Remember your goal is positive cash flow!

REAL WORLD CASH FLOW STATEMENT

(Numbers in parentheses indicate recommended percentages)

INCOME

Salary/Wages (net) _____
Investment Earnings _____

TOTAL INCOME (cash inflow) _____

CHARITABLE GIVING (5–10) _____

SAVINGS/INVESTMENTS (10–20) _____

Short-term _____
Long-term _____

DEBT/LOAN PAYMENTS (0–10) _____

Credit Cards _____
School Loans _____
Other _____

HOUSING (20–35)

Mortgage/Taxes/Rent _____
Repairs/Upkeep _____
Utilities (cable/electric/gas . . .) _____

TRANSPORTATION (5–15)

Car Loan _____
Gas/Maintenance/Repairs _____

INSURANCE (5)

Car _____
Home _____
Life _____
Medical _____

HOUSEHOLD/PERSONAL (15–25)

Food _____
Clothing _____
Liquor/Tobacco _____
Barber/Beauty/Massage _____
Technology _____
Books/Magazines _____
Gifts _____
Other _____

ENTERTAINMENT (5–10)

Dining _____
Shows _____
Vacations _____
Clubs/Rec. _____
Coffee/Social _____

MISCELLANEOUS (2–5) _____
TOTAL EXPENDITURES _____

TOTAL INCOME _____
LESS EXPENDITURES _____
NET CASH FLOW _____

BUDGETING

Now that you've seen how families analyze their spending through cash flow statements, the next step is creating a budget. This is an essential tool to ensure your spending remains within the targets you establish. In order to do a budget, you need to create "budgeted" or "targeted" levels of spending for each category that appears on the cash flow statement. (Note: the percentages appearing on the previous cash flow statements are a useful guide for determining budgeted amounts.) Then, by monitoring your actual spending (through keeping track of your expenses) you will be able to compare what you actually spent with the amounts you budgeted. The difference between actual and budgeted expenses is called a "variance," which will either be positive or negative depending on whether you over- or underspent compared to your budget.

Most people do budgets on a monthly or quarterly basis. If spending gets out of hand, it becomes very obvious from the budget worksheets. This will guide you to making the necessary adjustments to your lifestyle and spending in order to live within your means.

A sample budget form follows. Be sure to incorporate budgeting in your financial management. If everyone did, our world would be in much better financial shape!

Notes

_____

_____

_____

_____

_____

_____

_____

_____

_____

_____

_____

_____

_____

_____

_____

_____

BUDGET WORKSHEET

Period _____

CATEGORY	ACTUAL	BUDGET	VARIANCE	EXPLANATION
INCOME				
Salary/Wages (net)				
Investment Earnings				
TOTAL INCOME (cash inflow)				
CHARITABLE GIVING (5–10%)				
SAVINGS/INVESTMENTS (10–20%)				
Short-term				
Long-term				
DEBT/LOAN PAYMENTS (0–10%)				
Credit Cards				
School Loans				
Other				
HOUSING (20–35%)				
Mortgage/Taxes/Rent				
Repairs/Upkeep				
Utilities (cable/electric/gas . . .)				
TRANSPORTATION (5–15%)				
Car Loan				
Gas/Maintenance/Repairs				
INSURANCE (5%)				
Car				

What I
**Wish
I Knew**
at **18**

CATEGORY	ACTUAL	BUDGET	VARIANCE	EXPLANATION
Home				
Life				
Medical				
HOUSEHOLD/PERSONAL (15–25%)				
Food				
Clothing				
Liquor/Tobacco				
Barber/Beauty/Massage				
Technology				
Books/Magazines				
Gifts				
Other				
ENTERTAINMENT (5–10%)				
Dining				
Shows				
Vacations				
Clubs/Rec.				
Coffee/Social				
MISCELLANEOUS (2–5%)				
TOTAL EXPENDITURES				
TOTAL INCOME				
LESS EXPENDITURES				
NET CASH FLOW				

YOU'RE THE FINANCIAL ADVISOR!

Sean and Susie Spendthrift desperately need your help. They go "first class" in everything they do (finest restaurants/vacations/home/car/clothes) and were horrified to learn from their friendly banker that they failed to qualify for a loan. They were told, in no uncertain terms, that their spending has gotten out of control and they need to get their financial house in order.

The Spendthrifts never read *What I Wish I Knew at 18: Life Lessons for the Road Ahead* and have never produced a cash flow statement or measured their spending. As someone who has read the book and understands sound financial principles, you agree to offer your advice to get them back on track. You ask them to provide a list of expenses by category along with income, charitable donations, and investments.

Based on this information, you develop a cash flow statement and offer recommendations about how to turn their cash flow from negative to positive. In your interview, you learn that Susie has gone from a full-time web designer to part time (moving from $50,000 to $15,000 gross pay) in order to devote more time to volunteer causes. Sean is a contractor who grossed $57,000 last year. They're in a 25% tax bracket.

The listing of financial items and the blank Spendthrifts' Cash Flow Statement you will need to complete are on the following pages. Notice that each expenditure category has suggested percentages, which will assist you in developing your recommendations.

Be creative in your advice. The Spendthrifts need all the help they can get! Provide a summary assessment of their situation and detailed recommendations for them to consider.

Assessment and Recommendations

_____

_____

_____

_____

_____

_____

_____

_____

_____

_____

_____

SPENDTHRIFTS' FINANCIAL ITEMS (ANNUAL)

INCOME:

Combined salary (**gross**)	$72,000
Investment earnings	$0

CHARITABLE GIVING:

Local food bank:	$300

SAVINGS/INVESTMENTS:
(none available)

DEBT:

Credit cards (4)	$4,000
College loans	$2,500
Personal loan from friend	$500

HOUSING:

Mortgage	$15,000
Repairs, etc.	$1,000
Utilities	$3,000

TRANSPORTATION:

Autos	$7,200
Maintenance	$800

INSURANCE:

Car	$1,200
Home	$1,500
Life	$0
Medical	$1,000

HOUSEHOLD/PERSONAL:

Food	$8,000
Clothing	$2,700
Liquor/Tobacco	$800
Barber/Beauty/Massage	$700
Technology	$500
Books/Magazines	$200
Gifts	$800
Other	$0

ENTERTAINMENT:

Dining	$2,800
Coffee/Social	$800
Vacations	$2,500
Clubs/Rec.	$1,200

MISCELLANEOUS:	$1,500

ASSIGNMENT: FIX THE SPENDTHRIFTS' CASH FLOW

Using the following page, transfer the amounts from page 168 into the blank spaces on the cash flow statement below.

SPENDTHRIFTS' CASH FLOW STATEMENT

(Numbers in parentheses indicate recommended percentages)

INCOME
   Salary/Wages (net) _____
   Investment Earnings _____

TOTAL INCOME (cash inflow) _____

CHARITABLE GIVING (5–10) _____

SAVINGS/INVESTMENTS (10–20) _____
   Short-term _____
   Long-term _____

DEBT/LOAN PAYMENTS (0–10) _____
   Credit Cards _____
   School Loans _____
   Other _____

HOUSING (20–35)
   Mortgage/Taxes/Rent _____
   Repairs/Upkeep _____
   Utilities (cable/electric/gas . . .) _____

TRANSPORTATION (5–15)
   Car Loan _____
   Gas/Maintenance/Repairs _____

INSURANCE (5)
   Car _____
   Home _____
   Life _____
   Medical _____

HOUSEHOLD/PERSONAL (15–25)
   Food _____
   Clothing _____
   Liquor/Tobacco _____
   Barber/Beauty/Massage _____
   Technology _____
   Books/Magazines _____
   Gifts _____
   Other _____

ENTERTAINMENT (5–10)
   Dining _____
   Shows _____
   Vacations _____
   Clubs/Rec. _____
   Coffee/Social _____

MISCELLANEOUS (2–5) _____
TOTAL EXPENDITURES _____

TOTAL INCOME _____
LESS EXPENDITURES _____
NET CASH FLOW _____

What I
**Wish
I Knew** at **18**

ANSWERS TO FRIENDSHIP VERSES
EXERCISE FROM PAGE 47

1 Samuel 18:1–3	true, lasting friendship can occur suddenly
Proverbs 12:26	godly friends give good advice
Proverbs 16:28	gossip ruins friendships
Proverbs 17:17	faithful friends are a rare treasure
Proverbs 18:24	loyal friends love through difficult times
Proverbs 20:6	reliable friends are hard to find
Proverbs 22:11	purity and integrity gain the friendship of kings
Proverbs 22:24–25	the wrong friends can have a negative influence
Proverbs 27:5-6	sincere friends speak the truth in love, even when it hurts
Proverbs 27:9	counsel from a friend is pleasing
Proverbs 27:17	friends shape and sharpen one another
Ecclesiastes 4:9–12	true friends strengthen and help each other
John 15:13–15	friendship is marked by sacrifice
Proverbs 3:32	God is a friend to the godly
Romans 5:10	believers enjoy friendship with God
1 Corinthians 15:33	bad company corrupts good character
James 4:4	friendship with the world makes you an enemy of God

ANSWERS TO FINANCIAL VERSES
EXERCISE FROM PAGE 130

Deuteronomy 8:18	God is the source of our income/gives ability to produce wealth
Psalm 24:1	God owns everything; we should be wise stewards
Psalm 37:21	Repay debt promptly
Proverbs 3:9-10	Give God the first fruits of your income
Proverbs 22:7	Be cautious assuming debt; borrowers are servants to lenders
Ecclesiastes 11:2	Diversify your assets to reduce risk
Matthew 6:24	We can't serve two masters (God and money)
Luke 12:15	Guard against greed; life does not consist of one's possessions
Luke 19:12-27	Be productive with resources (invest to have your assets grow)
Acts 20:35	It is more blessed to give than receive
Romans 13:7-8	Repay debt promptly
Philippians 4:11-13	Be content with what we have
1 Timothy 6:6-8	Godliness with contentment is the greatest wealth

PRAYER JOURNAL

Date	Prayer Request	Impressions	Answer/Date